Malcolm MacColl

The Damnatory Clauses of the Athansian Creed

Malcolm MacColl

The Damnatory Clauses of the Athansian Creed
ISBN/EAN: 9783744700672

Printed in Europe, USA, Canada, Australia, Japan

Cover: Foto ©Lupo / pixelio.de

More available books at **www.hansebooks.com**

RIVINGTONS

London . *Waterloo Place*
Oxford . . *High Street*
Cambridge . . *Trinity Street*

THE

"DAMNATORY CLAUSES"

OF THE

ATHANASIAN CREED

RATIONALLY EXPLAINED

IN A LETTER

TO

THE RIGHT HON. W. E. GLADSTONE, M.P.

BY THE

REV. MALCOLM MACCOLL, M.A.

RECTOR OF ST. GEORGE, BOTOLPH LANE, WITH ST. BOTOLPH BY BILLINGSGATE

RIVINGTONS

London, Oxford, and Cambridge

1872

DEAR MR. GLADSTONE,

The real points at issue in the controversy on the Athanasian Creed have been so overlaid with irrelevant matter that it is not easy for the public at large to understand the exact position of the question. No doubt the debate in the Lower House of Convocation is well calculated to clear away a cloud of misapprehensions and errors on the subject. But the meagre reports of the debate that have been published in the secular press are worse than useless for that purpose, and the one or two Church papers which have given full reports are read by a comparatively select portion of the community. Something is still needed to place the question in its true bearings before the public mind, and the lull that is likely to follow the recent somewhat stormy discussion seems to offer a favourable opportunity to anyone who will venture to make the attempt. A great deal has been done already in this way by Mr. Brewer; but his two able Essays are confined chiefly, though not entirely, to the historical aspect of the question, and are addressed rather to the learned than to the popular mind. There is still room for a popular exposition of the true import of the Creed —popular at least so far as this, that nothing more than a very moderate education is required to follow the argument.

I trust that some one more competent than myself will apply his mind to the subject. In the meantime I offer the following pages as a humble contribution to so desirable an undertaking, and I have asked your kind permission to address them to you for two reasons: first, because the retention of the Athanasian Creed in the public service of the Church is alleged to be especially a layman's grievance; and secondly, because the question has an important political side to it in which statesmen can hardly fail to be interested. For it is now clear beyond all possibility of doubt, that a successful attempt either to mutilate the Creed or to degrade it from the position which it now occupies in the Prayer Book would have the effect of causing such a rent in the Church of England as would make the triumph of the Liberation Society a question of time, and of a very short time too. About thirty years ago Dr. Newman, in a letter to the late lamented Mr. Archer Butler, expressed his conviction that "our Church *could do anything*,* humanly speaking, if it knew its own strength, and if its members were at peace with each other." These words are true to-day. It is not the schemes of the Liberation Society which we have to fear, but the intestine strife which

---

* The italics are not mine.

reigns within our own borders; and no small part of this strife arises, I believe, from our mutual misunderstanding of each other. "Half the controversies in the world," says the same writer,* "are verbal ones, and could they be brought to a plain issue they would be brought to a prompt termination. Parties engaged in them would then perceive either that in substance they agreed together, or that their difference was one of first principles. This is the great object to be aimed at in the present age, though confessedly a very arduous one. We need not dispute, we need not prove, —we need but to define. At all events let us, if we can, do this first of all, and then see who are left for us to dispute with, what is left for us to prove. Controversy, at least in this age, does not lie between the hosts of heaven, Michael and his angels on the one side, and the powers of evil on the other; but it is a sort of night battle, where each fights for himself, and friend and foe stand together. When men understand what each other means, they see, for the most part, that controversy is either superfluous or hopeless."

It is impossible to read the Athanasian Creed debate in Convocation without recognizing the truth so felicitously expressed by Dr. Newman in this passage. It is, indeed, "a sort of night battle" where friends and foes are often mingled, and in which the combatants are

* 'University Sermons,' p. 192.

evidently either agreed in substance, or reason from premisses which are in their nature irreconcilable. The first thing that must be done, therefore, is to rid the question of all issues which are plainly irrelevant.

Conspicuous amongst these is the authorship of the Athanasian Creed, which has been pushed to the front in recent discussions on the subject, but which has really nothing to do with the question. "The single practical question," as the Bishop of St. David's truly observed,* "is this: whether we are or are not to continue the use of the Athanasian Creed in the public services of the Church; and I hold that with regard to this it is almost absurdly irrelevant to dwell on the authorship of the Creed. For my own part, I would say that if I were as firmly convinced that every syllable came from the pen of St. Athanasius as I am persuaded of the contrary, that would not in the slightest degree affect my objection to the continued use of the Creed in the services of the Church."† On the other hand, those who uphold the present position of the Creed would not be the least affected by the discovery that every word was composed centuries after St. Athanasius had slept with his fathers.‡ They

* See 'Guardian,' February 14, p. 208.
† Speech in Convocation. See 'Guardian' of February 14, 1872.
‡ What, by the way, is the Dean of Westminster's authority for asserting ('The Athanasian Creed,' p. 83) that "the Creed was received and enforced when it was believed to be 'the Creed of

regard the authorship of the Creed as a question of considerable literary interest, but of no practical importance whatever. So that if Mr. Ffoulkes's argument were as conclusive as it is manifestly and egregiously inconclusive, the Athanasian Creed would still rest on the prescriptive authority of Christendom for upwards of a thousand years.

Equally irrelevant with the authorship of the Athanasian Creed, as it appears to me, is the question of testing the accuracy of its text by the evidence of ancient manuscripts. In the case of Holy Scripture the testimony of ancient manuscripts is all-important, for the Church is but "the keeper of Holy Writ," and even an Œcumenical Council would have no authority to retain in the inspired Canon any passage that was clearly proved to be an interpolation. But the case of a Creed is altogether different. If the original manuscript of the Athanasian Creed were discovered, and were found to differ widely from the received text, it would not at all follow that the Creed ought to be amended into harmony with the manuscript. The Church accepts or rejects a disputed verse in the Bible on the ground of its being or not being an integral part of the original record; that consideration, and that only, suffices to decide the matter. But the

St. Athanasius'"? Is there any evidence to show that the compilers of the Prayer Book enjoined the use of the Athanasian Creed because they believed it to have been composed by St. Athanasius?

Church sanctions a Creed on the ground of its expressing her mind on the points with which it deals. And therefore if she takes up a form of words, and authorizes their use as a confession of faith, what matters it whether that form of words is, or is not, in agreement with ancient manuscripts? All that we have **to** consider is whether it is in truth the Creed which the Church has sanctioned. Grant, for the sake of argument, that it has been altered and enlarged. What then? So has the Apostles' Creed. Yet who would venture to propose any mutilation of the latter on the ground of its present form differing from some newly-discovered manuscript?

But we are told that the Athanasian Creed does not **rest** on Church authority at all, inasmuch as it has never received the sanction of a General Council. Are **we to** understand that all who object to the Creed would be satisfied if it could be proved to rest on the authority of a General Council? If they would not, the objection is not a sincere one; it is merely an *argumentum ad hominem,* intended to damage their opponents, but having no value in the eyes of those who **use** it. I am far from saying that arguments *ad hominem* are inadmissible in controversy; but in a discussion of this solemn nature it would certainly be convenient **if writers on** either side would restrict them**selves as much as possible to** arguments of which they would admit **the force if they were** used against them.

But, after all, it does not follow that the Athanasian Creed is deficient in authority because it lacks the direct sanction of a General Council. That argument would prove too much. It would be as fatal to the Apostles' as to the Athanasian Creed, and would even invalidate the authority of some parts of Holy Scripture. For the Bible, though appealed to in a general way, has never received the *imprimatur* of an Œcumenical Council book by book. General Councils meet for the purpose of condemning errors or settling disputed points; but it would be superfluous to call a General Council for the purpose of authorizing admitted truths and sanctioning points which were not disputed. If the Athanasian Creed were really so contrary to the spirit of the Gospel as its opponents would have us believe, we may be very sure that the mind of the Church would long ago have been declared against it.

Another argument against the Athanasian Creed is so extraordinary that I must quote it in the very words of one of its sponsors. "The recitation of this Creed," says the present Dean of Canterbury, "is a violation of Church principles, and condemned in the severest terms by the highest ecclesiastical authority. For the Church of England professes to receive the four first General Councils as next in authority to Holy Scripture, and accordingly the bishops of the whole Anglican Communion at the recent Lambeth Conference affirmed that they received the faith as defined by these Councils. But the Council of Constantinople in its seventh canon, and that of Chalcedon in the Definition of the Faith appended to its Acts, expressly forbid 'the composing, exhibiting, producing, or teaching of any other Creed.' For this they give a sufficient reason, namely, that the Nicene Creed, as finally settled at Constantinople, 'teaches completely the perfect doctrine concerning the Father, the Son, and the Holy Ghost, and fully explains the Incarnation of the Lord.' To guard more carefully against the imposition of new Creeds, they command that every bishop or clergyman so offending should be deposed, and every layman anathematized."

The first remark I have to make on this singular argument is that, if it can be **proved to be** valid, all the bishops and clergy of the Church of England, including Dr. Payne Smith, ought to be instantly deposed, "and every layman anathematized;" and this, not merely for using the Athanasian Creed, but for the additional offence of using the Constantinopolitan Creed, as they always do in the Communion Service. For it so happens that the Third General Council, that of Ephesus, prohibited the use of any other Creed than **that of** Nicæa in terms as stringent and peremptory **as those in** which **the** Fourth Council prohibited any other **Creed** than that of Constantinople.

The Ephesine fathers "decreed that it should be unlawful for any man to propose, or subscribe, or make any other Creed, *but what* **had** *been resolved upon by the holy fathers assembled at Nice,* with the Holy Ghost." And they went on to add that "they who dare to compose another Creed, or to introduce it, or offer it to them who are disposed to be converted to the knowledge of the truth from heathenism or Judaism, or any heresy whatsoever, should be deposed, if bishops, from the Episcopate; if priests, from the priesthood; and if laymen, that they should be anathematized."

It is not, I repeat, "the Nicene Creed as settled at Constantinople," but the Nicene Creed as settled at Nicæa, which is fenced round with these terrible safeguards. There is no room for doubt on this point, for the Nicene Creed, properly so called, is not only expressly mentioned in the canon, but is quoted at full length without the additions made to it by the Council of Constantinople in 381. If therefore the Dean of Canterbury's argument holds good, we are landed in this pleasant dilemma: we come under the anathema of the Council of Chalcedon for using "any other Creed" than "the Nicene Creed as settled at Constantinople," and we come under the anathema of the Council of Ephesus for using "any other Creed" than the "Nicene Creed as" *not* "settled at Constantinople."*

* Another inference from Dr. Payne Smith's argument is, that the anathemas which were appended to the original Nicene Creed ought to be still appended to it. If the prohibition against the use of "any other Creed" is directed against any expansion of the Creed,

Surely an argument which involves a *reductio ad absurdum* of so glaring a character as this refutes itself, and the wonder is that two Deans, who have filled respectively the Regius chairs of Divinity and Ecclesiastical History in the University of Oxford, should have committed themselves to so transparent a sophism. It is obvious that by the phrase " any other Creed " is not meant any orthodox addition to the Creed, either of Nicæa or Constantinople, but any different Creed—different in the sense of containing alien doctrine. The fathers of the Ephesine Council meant precisely what St. Paul meant when he anathematized all who should " preach any other **Gospel** " than that which the Galatians had received from him. **In fact, it is** not another *Creed*, but " another *faith* " ($\dot{\epsilon}\tau\acute{\epsilon}\rho\alpha\nu$ $\pi\acute{\iota}\sigma\tau\iota\nu$) which is forbidden. Any other interpretation would not only make the Fourth General Council contradict the Third, but would, in addition, **lay** such a yoke on the Church throughout all ages as even a General Council is not competent to impose. Neither the Fathers of Ephesus nor those of Chalcedon could foresee the needs of the Church throughout all time, and they had as little authority as they had inclination to forbid the imposition of a new Creed if circumstances required it. To add to the *confession* of the Church's faith is not to add

much more must it be directed against any curtailment of it. The Dean of Canterbury does not appear to be alive to the proverbial danger of playing with edged tools.

to the *faith,* for the faith admits of no addition. The Athanasian Creed is therefore not "another faith," but a fuller confession of the very faith which the Third and Fourth General Councils sought to guard by forbidding the substitution of any other. Besides, it is clear from the terms of the canon on which the Deans of Canterbury and Westminster rely that it was not the Church collectively which was forbidden to impose new Creeds, but only private individuals, who, of course, have no authority to impose any Creed, however orthodox, other than that which the Church has enjoined.

Another argument against the use of the Athanasian Creed in the public services of our Church, is founded on the allegation that "it is never recited in a mixed congregation in any other Church than our own."* If this assertion were ever so true, I am not sure that it would much strengthen the cause in behalf of which it has been enlisted. For granting, for the sake of argument, that the Athanasian Creed "is never recited in a mixed congregation in any other Church than our own," it is undeniable that the clergy of the Church of Rome are bound to recite it, on an average, about twenty-two times a year. But the proposal of the party of whom the Dean of Westminster is the most conspicuous champion is to relieve both clergy and laity from all obligation to read the Athanasian Creed at all. The

* 'The Athanasian Creed,' by the Dean of Westminster, p. 84. See also his speech in Convocation, 'Guardian,' May 1, p. 579.

argument would have some force if the proposal were to place the Creed on the same footing in the Church of England as it occupies in the Church of Rome; it loses its point altogether when urged in favour of degrading the Creed to a place below that which it occupies either in the Western or Eastern Church.

There has been a good deal of controversy **as to the exact place** occupied by the Athanasian Creed in the Church of Rome, and some eminent members of that Church, whom I have consulted on the point, do not give me precisely the same answer. I believe, however, that Dr. Newman has given a sufficiently clear statement of the case in the following passage, which I have his permission for quoting, in a letter which he **has** kindly written to me on the subject :—

"First, you must recollect we have nothing answering to the Anglican Prayer Book with you—no common prayer. Devotions are in great measure left to the private judgment of the individual. As to the Breviary, it is not, properly speaking, congregational at all. It is the solemn prayer of the clergy, the united prayer, said by each separately from the impracticability of saying it together, though such union is recommended, and actually said by them together in chapter, collegiate churches, monastic bodies, &c.

"Such public service the **laity** may attend, may join in,—in some countries, as in France, have been used to **join in.** But they might come to church while it went on, and say their own private prayers under (so to say) the shadow and in the power of it, joining in and with the Latin service, but using the while their own private prayers, under the feeling that all Christians are one, and have substantially the same words and petitions, and that their hearts are all open to God. They would join with the choir, as being helped by them and helping them also."

It is also true, as Dr. Newman informs me, that the book of private devotions, which has the special sanction of the Holy See (I mean the *Raccoltà*), does not contain the Athanasian Creed. "But further," I am quoting Dr. Newman, "in each country the local ecclesiastical authority not exactly provides, but sanctions, certain devotions. Hence we have various popular prayer books, of a miscellaneous character, containing prayers and offices for all classes of the faithful, and for all circumstances, such as the *Garden of the Soul*, &c. Now as to the French and Irish prayer books, some of them, as the *Key of Heaven* and the *Ursuline Manual*, do not contain the Athanasian Creed; but the English, all of them, do, *viz.* the *Garden of the Soul*, which dates from the time of Bishop Challoner, a century ago; the *Golden Manual*, the *Crown of Jesus*, and the *Path of Heaven*. The Athanasian Creed is in all these popular books, and the use, or at least the perusal and knowledge, of that Creed, is part of our good English tradition."

This "good English tradition," I am sorry to find, is

being encroached upon by foreign devotions of a less masculine type, and in some recent editions of the *Garden of the Soul* the Athanasian Creed is not to be found. I am told, however, that it is not omitted because there is any objection to it on the part either of the clergy or laity of the Roman Communion; it is simply elbowed out by devotions of a more emotional character. I may add, further, that more than one Roman Catholic priest, who have every right to speak on behalf of the sober catholicism of their Church, not only regret the encroachment on their old English devotions by foreign rivals, but would, moreover, be very glad to see the Athanasian Creed used generally in the public services of their Church. They believe, so one of them told me the other day, that their people suffer a great loss by seldom or never hearing the Creed in congregational worship;* and there are proposals in some quarters to insert it into the office of Benediction. So that at the very time some English churchmen are agitating for the extrusion of the Creed from the public service of our Church, some of the thoughtful members of the Church of Rome are proposing to restore it to the public service of their communion.

What, then, is the exact position occupied by the

* See M. Michaud's letter in the 'Guardian' of May 1, in which he laments the disuse of the Athanasian Creed among the Catholic laity of France, and traces it to the development of Ultramontanism.

Athanasian Creed in the Churches of England and Rome respectively? In the Church of England it is appointed to be used, at Morning Prayer, thirteen times a year; but out of these thirteen days there are only four on which the laity generally attend Morning Prayer. This must be qualified, however, by the admission that of the remaining nine days two, on an average in the course of the year, fall on a Sunday; so that the laity, as a body, are obliged to listen to or join in the recitation of the Athanasian Creed six times a year. The clergy are, of course, under obligation to use it thirteen times in the year, and the Eighth Article, moreover, binds them to accept its statements as implicitly as they do those of the Apostles' Creed or the Nicene. I am aware that this has been questioned of late, especially by the Bishop of St. David's, and I shall presently give some reasons why I think that his Lordship's opinions on that part of the subject cannot be sustained. But if they could be sustained they would weaken his case instead of strengthening it. He maintains, if I understand him aright, that absolute certainty is impossible in the sphere of religious truth; that contradictory statements in matters of faith are therefore equally admissible; and that consequently the "most certain warrants of Holy Scripture" predicated of the Athanasian Creed in the Eighth Article merely mean such warrants as appear certain to particular minds, and need not preclude a subscriber to the Article from conscientiously believing that the testimony of Holy Scripture is really against the Athanasian Creed.

This line of reasoning reduces subscription to a solemn mockery, but it also takes the sting out of the grievance which the Bishop of St. David's finds in the compulsory use of the Athanasian Creed. For if solemn language may be interpreted in the elastic sense for which the bishop contends, I do not see why the man who is obliged to recite the Athanasian Creed is in a worse case than the man who is obliged to sign the Eighth Article. The conscience which can subscribe without a twinge the proposition that the statements of the Athanasian Creed "may be proved by most certain warrants of Holy Scripture," and yet at the same time believes the contrary, need not, surely, be grievously shocked by the public recitation of a document to which he has already given his explicit sanction with a mental reservation. The Bishop of St. David's theory of interpretation has been compared with that of Dr. Newman in Tract XC. But there is really no analogy between the two cases. Dr. Newman contended that the popular interpretation of the Articles was not, or at least need not be, their real meaning, taking all the facts of the case into consideration; that, for instance, the doctrine of Purgatory condemned in one of the Articles does not mean every doctrine of purgatory, but only the "Romish doctrine." The reasons adduced by Dr. Newman in support of this view appear to me conclusive, and they have since been justified by the Judgment of the Judicial Committee of the Privy Council in the case of 'Essays and Reviews.' It is there decided that Mr. Wilson's doctrine of Purgatory is not inconsistent with faithful subscription to the Twenty-second Article, and the present Archbishop of Canterbury " is glad that the expression of such a hope" in Purgatory "is settled not to be actually punishable by the laws of our Church."*

This is very different from the Bishop of St. David's theory of interpretation. He maintains " that it will be found possible to prove by most certain warrant of Holy Scripture two propositions which are in direct conflict one with the other,"† and that therefore a subscriber to the Eighth Article may conscientiously maintain that the Athanasian Creed *cannot* " be proved by most certain warrants of Holy Scripture," and further, that " those portions which are the very essence of the Creed . . . ought never to have been made articles of faith." To compare this view of subscription with that advanced in Tract XC. is simply absurd. The one maintains that the Thirty-nine Articles are historically and grammatically capable of a catholic interpretation; the other asserts that two distinctly contradictory interpretations of the Articles are equally tenable, since truth is relative to the individual, and not absolute in

---

* See Preface to his 'Sermons on the Word of God and the Ground of Faith.'

† See his speech in Convocation, 'Guardian,' February 14, p. 208.

itself. In other words, the theory of the Bishop of St. David's is founded on Pyrrhonism pure and simple, while that of Dr. Newman merely maintains that the popular gloss on the Thirty-nine Articles does not represent their true meaning. I cannot help expressing my regret that the Bishop of St. David's should have been a party to the hounding of Dr. Newman out of the Church of England a quarter of a century ago for putting forth a view of the Thirty-nine Articles which is mildness itself compared with that which the Bishop himself has now propounded.

But to return to the place which the Athanasian Creed occupies respectively in the Churches of England and of Rome. In the Church of England the laity, as a body, are obliged to recite or listen to it about six times a year. The clergy are bound to recite it thirteen times a year, and to acknowledge, in addition, that it "ought thoroughly to be received and believed," because it "may be proved by most certain warrants of Holy Scripture."

In the Church of Rome the clergy are bound to say the Athanasian Creed about twenty-two times a year. The office in which it occurs is, in theory, an office for united worship, and is used as such in cathedral, collegiate, and monastic establishments. Practically, however, the laity seldom attend the office of Prime, and have, indeed, but few opportunities of doing so; and consequently they rarely hear the Athanasian Creed in the service of the Church. On the other hand, there is no question in the Church of Rome as to the Athanasian Creed being untrue or uncharitable, or unsuited for lay use. On the contrary, it is found in nearly all the books of devotion recommended by the Church for the use of the laity in this country. "That it is the authoritative word of the Church," Dr. Newman tells me, "and the infallible answer of the Church to all her children who ask questions on the subject of which it speaks, is quite certain."

In both the Roman and Anglican Churches, therefore, the Athanasian Creed holds at present an authoritative and a dogmatic position. In the Church of Rome the use of the Creed is binding on the clergy with far greater stringency than it is on ours, but the use of it is not imperative on the laity at all.* In both Churches it is a dogmatic standard of appeal for clergy and laity on the questions of which it treats; but it is evident that it would lose its dogmatic position in the Church of England if any of the chief proposals lately made respecting it should be carried into effect.

1. The proposal most in vogue during the past twelvemonth, and which has been fathered on the Bishop of Winchester, is that the Creed should be

---

* Nor is it on our laity. The only Creed which is, properly speaking, *imposed* on our laity is the Apostles' Creed.

taken out of the Prayer Book and buried among the Thirty-nine Articles. This proposal was advocated at a public meeting in St. James's Hall, by Mr. Cowper Temple, the Bishop of Exeter, Dean Stanley, Dr. Barry, Dr. Miller, and others, and was carried by a large majority. There is no need, however, to discuss it now. It found no advocate in Convocation, even Dean Stanley expressed his contempt for it afterwards, and its putative parent has scornfully disowned it.

2. Another proposal is to make the Creed optional, either by putting "may" instead of "shall" in the rubric which prescribes its use; or by leaving it to the discretion of the officiating minister to use it on the appointed days instead of the Apostles' Creed. This is a trifle less degrading to the Creed than its banishment among the Thirty-nine Articles; but the proposal is both illogical and mischievous. If the Creed "savours of heresy," as Canon Swainson asserts, or is "avowedly heretical," as the Dean of Westminster assures us, or is terribly uncharitable and unchristian, as all who agitate for its abolition declare, it is surely a strange remedy to leave every parish priest in England free to use it or not, as his fancy dictates. Would the laity who object to the Creed consider it less objectionable if it were imposed upon them by the private judgment of a single clergyman rather than by the authority of the Church? I have naturally a great respect for the clergy of the Church of England; but I protest against

our being empowered to impose our own opinions as articles of faith on the laity. For it is evident that under an optional system the clergyman who read and he who omitted the Creed would alike be imposing their own opinions on the laity, and the Creed would thus be robbed of all dogmatic authority. It would no longer be what Dr. Newman says it is in the Church of Rome, "the authoritative word of the Church, and her infallible answer to all her children who ask questions on the subjects of which it speaks." I can now refer to the Athanasian Creed as an authoritative exposition of the faith; but I can do so no longer if the Church of England should authorize its disuse on the ground of some of its clauses being both false and unchristian. And the proposal would prove to be not less mischievous than illogical. In truth it would be difficult to devise a plan better calculated to set clergy and laity by the ears. If an ill-instructed layman here and there sits down and shuts his book with a bang when the Creed is said on the authority of the Church, what would be the measure of his indignation when it was said on the private authority of the parson? The optional use of the Creed would, in fact, introduce the seeds of strife into almost every parish in England; a curious result certainly from the labours of a Royal Commission which was appointed for the express purpose of bringing about a more uniform observance of the rubrics of the Prayer Book.

3. The third proposal is to mutilate the Athanasian Creed—to cut out of it the clauses which give offence to some persons. This is a proposal which, I hold, lies absolutely beyond the competency of the Church of England. At present, notwithstanding all that has been said to the contrary, the Athanasian Creed is an exposition of the Catholic faith, accepted as such by the whole of Christendom. Mutilate it, and it ceases to be the Athanasian Creed; it becomes a new and a different confession of faith. All that has been said about the "damnatory clauses" being only "the setting" of the Creed is mere rubbish. They belong to its essence, and are, in fact, implied in all Creeds. Why is any Creed necessary if belief in it is, after all, a matter of indifference? And belief in it must be a matter of indifference if the principle of the "damnatory clauses" is repudiated. I repeat, therefore, that the excision of the "damnatory clauses" would make the Athanasian Creed a new Creed; and the advocates of mutilation are thus landed in a strange inconsistency. They object to the Creed because it is not older, as they think, than the time of Charlemagne; and by way of remedy they propose to make it as modern as the time of Queen Victoria. They wish to abolish it because it is not old enough; and they propose to retain it on condition that it can be made less old than it is! They think it ought not to be used in the public services of the Church, though it has the approval of Christendom, because it has not

the express sanction of an Œcumenical Council; but they think it would be right to use it in the public services of the Church if it were mutilated into a shape which has never been sanctioned by any portion of the Catholic Church.

4. The fourth proposal, and the last which I shall notice here, is that of leaving the Athanasian Creed as it is in the Prayer Book, but abolishing the rubric which prescribes its use. This, of course, would be equivalent to a prohibition against its use; and if it is forbidden to be used, I see no reason why it should be retained in the Prayer Book at all.

I have now noticed the only proposals which, as far as I know, have been seriously entertained by those who dislike the Athanasian Creed, and it is obvious that the effect of adopting any of them would be to deprive the Creed of all dogmatic authority, and to degrade it below the place which it occupies throughout the rest of Christendom. In the Church of Rome and in the Eastern Church the Athanasian Creed is acknowledged as a dogmatic rule of faith. It was adopted as such by the English Church at the Reformation, and also by all continental reformers. "Lutherans, Zuinglians, and Calvinists, vied with each other in their adoption of the Athanasian Creed."[*] What is now proposed, therefore, is not to put the

[*] Palmer's 'Treatise on the Church of Christ,' i., p. 98.

Creed on the same footing which it occupies in other Communions, but to put an indignity upon it which neither the Church of Rome nor the Eastern Church would endure for a moment. And yet we are seriously asked to believe that the degradation or mutilation of the Athanasian Creed would greatly facilitate the reunion of Christendom. The difference between ourselves and the Church of Rome—and the same may be said of the Eastern Church—in the use of the Athanasian Creed is a difference of method, not of principle.* I quote Dr. Newman again: "It is no sound argument that you should remove it from your Common Prayer because we haven't it in our Common Prayer, *for we have no united vocal Common Prayer.* You might as well say that you should leave out the Ten Commandments because we have not the Ten Commandments read in Church; for we have no imperative Common Prayers such as yours. The Athanasian Creed *is* imposed upon our clergy." This pertinent observation is equally true of the Eastern Church. It has "no united vocal Common Prayer." But the Athanasian Creed is in the Horologium; and it is in books of devotion recommended for the use of the laity. Clearly, therefore, no valid argument for the disuse of the Athanasian Creed

* The Senior Professor of Theology in Maynooth College, Dr. Murray, allows me to state, on his authority, that "the Church (of Rome) is fully committed to the perfect purity of each doctrinal statement in the Athanasian Creed, just as much as if that purity had been defined by a General Council."

can be drawn from the practice of the Greek or Roman Church, and all that has been spoken or written on that point may be dismissed as irrelevant rhetoric.

I am far from asserting, however, that under other circumstances, it might not be advisable to modify in some degree the obligation to use the Athanasian Creed; as, for instance, among some of our mining population, who "are become such as have need of milk, and not of strong meat." In such cases I see no reason, abstractedly, why the Ordinary should not be empowered to dispense an incumbent from the obligation to use the Creed till such time as his people were sufficiently instructed to digest "strong meat."* But no concession which did not go farther than this would satisfy those who dislike the Creed, and any concession would certainly be misunderstood at this time. The most conspicuous assailants of the Creed have been very careful to assure us that they do not object to it because they think it too strong meat for such as are

---

* I am obliged to say that I offer even this suggestion with considerable diffidence; for it is a very remarkable fact that every missionary bishop in Convocation insisted on the value of the Athanasian Creed even in the case of neophytes. Bishop Claughton found it useful among the natives of Ceylon, Bishop M'Dougall among his Chinese converts in Borneo, and the Bishop of Lichfield among the Maories of New Zealand. The late Bishop Cotton, too, having gone to India with some prejudices against the use of the Athanasian Creed, found it so valuable as an antidote against the various forms of Oriental theosophy, that he became one of the most earnest advocates for its use in congregational worship.—See Appendix, Note A.

"babes" in religious knowledge, but because they think it untrue and uncharitable. This was the ground taken up by Dean Stanley, whom even those who differ from him most must admire for the fearless honesty with which he always accepts the full consequences of his premisses. He declared the other day, in his place in Convocation, that the "damnatory clauses" **in the** Athanasian Creed were "absolutely false;" and in **his** little book* on the subject he affirms emphatically that **the** Athanasian Creed, "so far from recommending the doctrine of the Trinity to unwilling minds, is the chief **obstacle** in the way of the acceptance of that doctrine."†

* 'The Athanasian Creed,' p. 85.

† Dr. Swainson uses language equally strong and somewhat more offensive in his speech in Convocation. "With regard to the last clause, he had no hesitation in saying that it was false, and it was time for it to be altered. Whatever explanations were put upon it, they were not the meaning which the words conveyed. They were explaining away, and a thing that wanted explaining away ought not to be kept. . . . . This was not a time to speak smoothly, and therefore he would say it was because he held the clause to be, literally speaking, untrue, that he objected to hear in the documents of the Church of England expressions which required such explanations."—'Guardian,' April 24, p. 535. Since Dr. Swainson thinks that "this is not a time to speak smoothly," I hope he will forgive me for asking, who is Dr. Swainson that he should lay down the law in this dictatorial manner, making his own mind, forsooth! the rule and measure of all human intelligence? When the intellect of Dr. Swainson is on one side and the intellect of Christendom for centuries on the other, I hope it is not very presumptuous to believe that Dr. Swainson's interpretation of the Athanasian Creed is possibly an erroneous one.

To make any concession at the present moment, therefore, would be to acknowledge the justice of the Dean's strictures, and to proclaim to the world that the Athanasian Creed contains propositions which are "absolutely false," and an obstacle in the way of those who would otherwise willingly accept the doctrine of the Trinity.

But it is worth while, in passing, to examine the Dean of Westminster's startling statement a little more closely. He asserts that the Athanasian Creed, "so far from recommending the doctrine of the Trinity to unwilling minds, is the chief obstacle in the way of the acceptance of that doctrine." Doubtless the Dean knows what he says, and must have facts to support him. But I am inclined to think that his experience is a very exceptional one. Mine, at all events, is of a contrary character. I have been told by more than one Nonconformist that they have found the Athanasian Creed a great help in laying hold of the doctrine of the Trinity. A great deal depends, however, on the meaning which we attach to the word Trinity, and I do not feel quite sure that I understand the sense in which the Dean uses it in the above passage. "Emmanuel Swedenborg," he tells us,* "and his followers, who acknowledge no Person in the Trinity but that of 'the Divine Man Jesus Christ,' are yet ardent admirers of the Athanasian Creed, and claim its

* 'The Athanasian Creed,' p. 22.

sanction for their doctrine, and are ready to 'demonstrate that all its contents, even to the very words, are agreeable to the truth, *provided* * that for a Trinity of Persons we understand a Trinity of Person'"—provided, that is, we suffer the doctrine of the Trinity to evaporate in the shadowy counterfeit of it which Sabellianism offers in its place. "With this reservation," the Dean of Westminster goes on to say, quoting White's 'Life of Swedenborg,' "the mind of a Swedenborgian may traverse the clauses of that arduous dogma with joyful assent and consent." Doubtless; for the reservation in question gives us, not a Trinity of Persons, but a triune manifestation of one Person. No doubt the Athanasian Creed "is the chief obstacle in the way of the acceptance of *that* doctrine." But the doctrine of the Trinity which the Dean of Westminster and I hold is very different. We believe that the Trinity of the Christian Creed does not mean a succession of characters assumed by one Person in the sphere of time, but a distinction of Persons whose relations to each other are coincident and eternal. I wonder the Dean did not see that his quotation from Swedenborgian theology is, in fact, a striking tribute to the value of the Athanasian Creed as a bulwark of the Christian doctrine of the Trinity. Swedenborg could accept the "arduous dogma" of the Trinity in a Sabellian sense, "*provided*" the Athanasian Creed were abolished or altered. Just so. And there-

* The italics are the Dean's.

fore I trust that the Athanasian Creed will neither be abolished nor altered. To do either, in response to this challenge, would be to abandon the faith and commit the Church of England to Sabellianism.

I cannot see much in the argument that the Athanasian Creed ought to be disused because some distinguished names have at different times objected to it, for a much larger number of names still more distinguished could easily be marshalled on the other side. Still, if the Athanasian Creed is to be thrown down by having great names flung at it, care should be taken that none but fairly legitimate names are summoned for that purpose; and this caution is especially necessary in the case of persons who are no longer on earth to defend themselves. The Dean of Westminster has, I think, been a little hasty in this respect. He has quoted Chillingworth's strong language in 1635, namely, that "the damning clauses in St. Athanasius' Creed are most false, and also in a high degree schismatical and presumptuous;" but he has forgotten to add that Chillingworth practically retracted this opinion three years afterwards. In the year 1635 Chillingworth refused to sign the Thirty-nine Articles, partly on account of the "damnatory clauses" in the Athanasian Creed, and partly because he did not think the Fourth Commandment binding on Christians. But, "upon more mature consideration," as Waterland says, " he happily got over his difficulties and subscribed," in the following terms :—

Ego Gulielmus Chillingworth, **Clericus,** in Artibus Magister, ad Cancellariatum **Ecclesiæ** Cathedralis Beatæ Mariæ Sarum, **una cum Præbenda de Brinworth,** alias Brickleworth, in Comitatu Northampton **Petriburgensis** Diœceseos in **eadem** Ecclesia fundata, **et eidem Cancel**lariatui annexa, admittendus et instituendus, *omnibus hisce Articulis, et Singulis in eis contentis, volens* **et ex** *animo subscribo, et consensum meum eisdem præbeo.* Vicesimo die Julii, 1638. *Gulielmus Chillingworth.*

It is a mistake, therefore, **to quote** Chillingworth against the Athanasian **Creed. If he is** to be cited at all, he is rather **a witness for the defence,** unless it be maintained that he **was** a hypocrite **when he** signed the Articles, in which case **his** opinion would be worthless on either side. For surely the adhesion, *ex animo* and " after mature consideration," of a man who condemned the Athanasian Creed in such unqualified language, **is** a much more striking testimony to its value than that of one who never doubted. **If** Chillingworth had never **retracted his** adverse opinion, opposed **as it is to** the *consensus* of Christendom, that fact **would not** influence my judgment in the slightest degree. **But** those who think much of his passionate **invective** against the Athanasian Creed ought to be still more impressed by his subsequent acceptance of it *volens et ex animo.* Is it not possible, moreover, that if they follow his example and enter on a dispassionate and "mature consideration" of the Creed, they, too, may be able in the course of three years to regard it with different feelings? And this is one good reason why **Convocation should have decided against precipitate legislation.**

Another name which the Dean of Westminster presses into his service is that of Baxter. It is not an authoritative name on such a subject; but, *quantum valeat,* the real drift of his testimony is rather against the Dean of Westminster than for him. It is true he had an objection to the "damnatory clauses," but he would have been quite satisfied with such an explanatory note as, for instance, the Oxford Professors have suggested. His words are, "the damnatory clauses excepted, *or modestly expounded,* I embrace the Creed commonly called Athanasius' *as the best explanation of the Trinity.*" And elsewhere, "I unfeignedly account the doctrine of the Trinity the sum and kernel of the Christian religion, as expressed in our baptism and Athanasius' Creed, *the best exposition of it I ever read.*" I humbly submit, therefore, that Baxter cannot fairly be quoted, any more than Chillingworth, by those who would banish the Athanasian Creed from the public services of the Church. It is to be observed, too, that this eminent leader of Nonconformity found the Athanasian Creed the reverse of "an obstacle in the way of his acceptance of the doctrine of the Trinity."

Jeremy Taylor is undoubtedly a greater name than Baxter or even Chillingworth, and both the Dean of Westminster and the Bishop of St. David's have accordingly not failed to invoke his aid against the Athanasian Creed. It may be questioned, however, whether his alliance in this matter is not more damaging than his hostility would have been. For charm of diction, affluence of imagination, and the fervour of his devotional writings, Jeremy Taylor will always occupy a distinguished place in our literature. But whoever wants accuracy of theological thought and expression must seek it elsewhere than in the works of Jeremy Taylor. He had something like a passion for running his head against all articles of faith which placed any check on the wanderings of an unusually discursive imagination, and as a controversialist he was not always very scrupulous; nor had he, when the mood was upon him, any objection to "damnatory clauses" of his own, in comparison with which those of the Athanasian Creed are mild indeed.* A writer who could

---

* "Jeremy Taylor, in two singularly unrhetorical and unimpassioned chapters, deliberately enumerates the most atrocious acts of cruelty in human history, and says that they are surpassed by the tortures inflicted by the Deity. A few instances will suffice. Certain persons 'put rings of iron, stuck fast with sharp points of needles, about their arms and feet, in such a manner as the prisoners could not move without wounding themselves; then they compassed them about with fire, to the intent that, standing still they might be burned alive, and if they stirred the sharp points pierced their

characterize the Arian controversy contemptuously as a dispute about a vowel, and who held himself at liberty to accept or reject the Nicene Creed, is not likely to be owned as an authority on matters of faith by those who believe, as the Church throughout the world has always believed, that the very life of Christianity depended on the definition of Nicæa. To say that it makes no difference whether we consider the Son as ὁμοούσιος or as ὁμοιούσιος with the Father, is simply to say that it matters not whether we believe in the Trinity or not. For if the Son is not consubstantial with the Father, He is either a creature or another God: a creature, if

---

flesh. . . . . What, then, shall be the torment of the damned where they burn eternally without dying, and without the possibility of removing? . . . . Alexander, the son of Hyrcanus, caused eight hundred to be crucified, and whilst they were yet alive caused their wives and children to be murdered before their eyes, that so they might not die once, but many deaths. This rigour shall not be wanting in hell. . . . . Mezentius tied a living body to the dead until the putrefied exhalations had killed the living. . . . . What is this in respect of hell, when each body of the damned is more loathsome and unsavoury than a million of dead dogs? . . . . Bonaventure says, if one of the damned were brought into this world it were sufficient to infect the whole earth. . . . . We are amazed to think of the inhumanity of Phalaris, who roasted men alive in his brazen bull. That was a joy in respect of that fire of hell. . . . . The torment . . . . comprises as many torments as the body of man has joints, sinews, arteries, &c., being caused by that penetrating and real fire, of which this temporal fire is but a painted fire. . . . . What comparison will there be between burning for an hundred years' space, and to be burning without interruption as long as God is God?' ('Contemplations on the State of Man,' book ii., ch. 6-7.)"—Lecky's 'History of European Morals,' ii., p. 239.

He is of a created substance; another God, if His substance is uncreated, yet not identical with the Father's.

With his looseness of view on this point, it is no wonder that Jeremy Taylor wrote disparagingly of the Nicene as well as of the Athanasian Creed; but surely the very fact of his having done so ought to have disqualified him as a witness in this controversy. The Bishop of St. David's, however, is of a different opinion. **He** thinks that Jeremy Taylor "is a person whose opinions are entitled to very considerable respect;" and it must be owned that the respect which his Lordship does pay to them is even more than "considerable." He actually **seems to** have persuaded himself that the single authority of Jeremy Taylor **is** sufficient to outweigh the decision of a General Council. Nor is this a mere hasty opinion uttered on the spur of the moment in the heat of debate, for **the** Bishop repeats it deliberately in a letter to the 'Guardian' of April **10.** "In my speech in Convocation," he says, **"I** drew attention **to** the fact that, in Jeremy Taylor's view, it was a **matter open to** very grave doubt whether the Council of Nicæa was justified, in point of discretion, in framing **any new** Creed at all. He himself clearly thought that it would have been better to have 'kept the very words of Scripture,' and **not to have** introduced such a term as ὁμοούσιος." No doubt that **was** Jeremy Taylor's opinion, and for that very reason it appears to me "a matter open **to** very **grave** doubt whether" an opinion so subversive of the dogmatic position of the Church of England ought to have been quoted with approbation by a Bishop of that Church. The plain truth seems to be that the Bishop of St. David's has relied too much on the native acuteness of his intellect, and has not taken the trouble to acquaint himself with the real attitude of the Church of England in respect to the authority of the General Councils. His off-hand reference to the Twenty-first Article proves this. "If," he says, "the Article which requires us to believe that 'General Councils may err, and sometimes have erred, even in things pertaining to God,' sanctions such a judgment in a Creed promulgated by a General Council, much more must we be at liberty to hold a like opinion with regard to the composition of any private Doctor, even if it was Athanasius himself."

With the leave of the Bishop of St. David's, I humbly venture to deny that the Twenty-first Article gives any such sanction as he imagines to Jeremy Taylor's flippant "judgment on a Creed promulgated by a General Council." The truth is, "General Council" is an equivocal phrase. It covers the Creed of Nicæa; but it may also cover the Creed of Ariminum. A General Council, in its idea, is an assembly in which all the Sees of Christendom are represented. But no such Council has ever taken place. In the era of the Arian controversy the number of Sees in East and West together was about two thousand, and of these only a moiety were represented in the first six General Councils, whose decrees are accepted by the Church universal. The Council of Nicæa numbered only three hundred and eighteen Bishops, that of Ephesus about two hundred, and that of Constantinople only one hundred and fifty; in other words, the number of bishops present at the first three Œcumenical Councils respectively were about one-thirteenth, one-ninth, and one-sixth of the whole Episcopate. On the other hand, several Councils whose decisions have been rejected by the Church were much more representative as regards numbers than most of those whose decrees, as the Church of England declares, " are allowed and received of all men." The Arianising Council of Ariminum was attended by four hundred bishops, and Eutychianism prevailed in a Council consisting of above six hundred.

It is evident, therefore, that we cannot predicate inerrancy beforehand of any Council; for it is not the number of bishops present, but the consent of the Church dispersed throughout the world, that confers on the decrees of any Council an œcumenical character. It is of course morally impossible that the collective mind of Christendom, if it found a truly representative organ, could go astray in a matter of faith; for otherwise our Lord's promise would fail, " and the gates of hell" would indeed " prevail against " His Church. But whether the collective mind of the Church at large is fairly represented in any particular Council can only be ascertained by the consent of the Church afterwards. A Council whose decrees, on being made known throughout the world, are accepted by the Church universal as the expression of its faith, receives thereby an œcumenical character, and its decrees are universally binding. On the other hand, a Council, however general in the composition and number of its members, whose decrees fail to command this universal assent, is not really œcumenical ; and it may be truly said of it not only that it " may err," but that it "has erred" in fact.

This is a distinction which is quite familiar to theological students, and I am surprised that the Bishop of St. David's should have overlooked it. "The final authority of proper œcumenical synods," says Palmer,* "does not arise merely from the number of bishops assembled in them, but from the approbation of the Catholic Church throughout the world ; which, having received their decrees, examines them with the respect due to so considerable an authority, compares them with Scripture and Catholic tradition, and by an universal approbation and execution of those decrees, pronounces a final and irrefragable sentence in their favour." This is certainly the view of the Gallican School of Roman Catholic divines. They all declare that the consent of the Church dispersed is necessary to the validity of all conciliar decrees. The following authorities are quoted by Palmer :—

* 'Treatise on the Church,' ii., p. 151.

De Barral, Archbishop of Tours, says, "These are facts which prove in an invincible manner that neither the decrees of Popes nor even those of Councils acquire an irrefragable authority except by virtue of the consent of the Universal Church." "The last mark of any Council or assembly's representing truly the Catholic Church," says Bossuet, "**is when** the whole body of the Episcopate, and the whole **society** which professes to receive its instructions, approve and receive this Council; this, I say, is the last seal of the authority of this Council, and the infallibility of its decrees." Again, "The Council of Orange . . . was by no means universal. It contained chapters which the Pope had sent. In this Council there were scarcely twelve or thirteen bishops; but because it was received without opposition its decisions are no more disputed than those of the Council of Nice, *because everything depends on consent.* There were but few bishops of the West in the Council of Nice, there were none in that of Constantinople, none in that of Ephesus, and at Chalcedon only the legates of the Pope; and the same may be said of others. But *because all the world consented then or afterwards* those decrees are the decrees of the whole world. . . . If we go farther back, Paul of Samosata was condemned only by a particular Council held at Antioch; but because its decree was addressed to all the bishops in the world and received by them (*for in this resides the whole force,* and **without** it the mere address would be nothing), this decree is immoveable."

These are specimens of the teaching of the moderate school in the Church of Rome, and Palmer is amply justified in saying that "it is now generally affirmed by Roman Catholic theologians of respectability, after Bossuet, that the only final proof of the œcumenicity of a Council is its acceptance by the Universal Church as œcumenical; and that this acceptance confers on it such an authority that no defects in its mode of celebration can be adduced afterwards to throw doubt on its judgments." Nor is the distinction here insisted on confined to writers of Bossuet's school. The Ultramontane Bellarmine* divides *Generalia Concilia* into *Generalia Concilia approbata, Generalia Concilia reprobata; Generalia Concilia partim approbata, partim reprobata; Generalia Concilia nec manifeste probata, nec manifeste reprobata.* So that, in the opinion of Bellarmine, a Council might be "general" and yet err, and he enumerates several General Councils whose decrees have been repudiated by the Church, and which therefore must be considered to have erred.

That this is the sense of the Twenty-first Article is evident, because the Church of England acknowledges, in the Second Book of Homilies, the authority of "those six Councils *which were allowed and received of all men.*" And an Act of Parliament declares that "nothing is

* 'De Conciliis Ecclesiæ,' lib. i., c. 5-8.

to be adjudged heresy but that which heretofore has been so adjudged by the authority of the Canonical Scriptures, *or the first four General Councils, or some other General Council,* wherein the same hath been declared heresy by the express words of Scripture."*
Moreover, in her Canons of 1571, the Church of England expressly enjoins her clergy to be careful "that they never teach aught in a sermon, to be religiously held and believed by the people, but what is agreeable to the doctrine of the Old or New Testament, and which the Catholic Fathers and ancient Bishops have collected from that very doctrine." This Canon was framed nine years after the publication of the Thirty-nine Articles, and by the same hands; and it supplies us therefore with the meaning which the Twenty-first Article bore in the minds of those who composed it. It is clear that they accepted the authority of "those six General Councils which were allowed and received of all men," as final, and their decrees as irrevocable. In fact, there is no reasonable doubt that the Twenty-first Article was aimed at the Council of Trent, which was then sitting. It was a declaration beforehand that its decrees would not be considered binding by the Church of England. Jeremy Taylor, therefore, in claiming the right of sitting in judgment on the Nicene Council, simply repudiated the authority of the Church from which he received

* 1 Eliz., cap. i., A.D. 1558.

his commission; and the Bishop of St. David's, in backing him up, is amenable to the same observation.

So far I have been dealing with matters which, though imported into the discussion on the Athanasian Creed, do not really touch the essence of the controversy. The Athanasian Creed, after all, is not assailed because its reputed authorship is doubtful or spurious, or because the Church of England makes a more prominent use of it than other Churches, or because various names, great and small, have at different times objected to it, or because its technical language makes it unsuitable for use in mixed congregations, or because it never received the sanction of an Œcumenical Council; but because it asserts, in language too plain to be misunderstood or explained away, that wilful perversion of the Christian faith is as perilous to men's everlasting interests as wilful transgression of the moral law. The "damnatory clauses" are the real rock of offence, and the assailants of the Creed will be appeased by no concession which stops short either of their excision or of the abrogation of the compulsory use of the Creed. Now, for my own part, I will say frankly that the "damnatory clauses" have never presented the smallest difficulty to my mind. I have always repeated them *ex animo* and without the least hesitation or compunction; and yet I do not think that my natural disposition is exceptionally cruel or even intolerant; nor do I admit, on the other hand, that I interpret the Creed in any non-natural sense whatever. I apply to it the same rules of interpretation which men in general apply to the Bible or to Blackstone's 'Commentaries,' and I accept it in as literal a sense as the Apostles' Creed **or the** Nicene. Suffer me then to put down in plain language what **I conceive** to be the natural and obvious meaning of the so-called " damnatory clauses."

" Whosoever will be saved, before all things it is necessary that he hold the Catholic faith, which faith except everyone do keep whole and undefiled, without doubt he shall perish everlastingly."

Terrible words certainly. What do they mean? Unquestionably they must be understood as meaning that an Arian, for example, or Sabellian, or Nestorian or any other proved heretic, " shall perish everlastingly." This is the plain and obvious meaning, and any interpretation short of it must be rejected as absolutely irreconcilable with the language of the Creed. But having admitted so much, I proceed to draw an important distinction. To say " an Arian shall perish everlastingly" is **a very** different proposition from saying " Arius **shall** perish everlastingly." And if anyone thinks that this is **a** subtle distinction, and, in fact, a mere playing with words, we can easily test the validity of my explanation by transferring the question from the region of theology to that of morals. Is there no difference between saying "a murderer shall perish everlastingly" and saying "Marguerite Dixblanc, the Park Lane murderess, shall perish everlastingly." Clearly there is, and everybody admits it. The former is an abstract proposition. It denounces a certain punishment against a certain crime, and the denunciation is in a personal form, since of course a crime necessarily supposes a criminal. But the criminal is denounced *quâ* criminal, and not *quâ* man. The crime is personified, and judgment is passed upon it accordingly. Murder is inadmissible in heaven, and therefore no murderer, *as such*, can be admitted there. But man is a complex being, and we cannot be sure that any specific offence against faith or morals is a true index to his character as a whole. It is the key in which the thoughts habitually move that determines the condition of man as a responsible moral agent, and God alone, Who sees the heart, can know for certain what that key is. The sum total of man's capacities for everlasting life are not necessarily exhausted by the few gross acts incident to social relations or open to human valuation; but it is on such acts alone that human judgments can be passed, as well in the sphere of faith as in that of morals. The Church solemnly warns her children that as there is but one "straight and narrow way that leadeth unto life," wilful deviation from that way leads to perdition; but she does not point to any individual human being and say, "*thou* art the man, *thou* shalt perish everlastingly." St. Paul, for example, lays it down as an axiom of the Christian religion that certain gross sins exclude the sinner from heaven. "*Ye know* that no whoremonger, nor unclean person, nor covetous man who is an idolater, hath any inheritance in the kingdom of Christ and of God." This is another way of saying that such offenders "shall perish everlastingly," for exclusion from the kingdom of God is perdition. And this is quite true in the abstract. No unclean person, *as such,* has any inheritance in the kingdom of God. But did the Apostle intend that his universal proposition should have a particular application? In other words, did he mean that any Ephesian offender in particular should "perish everlastingly"? No one will think so. The unclean Ephesian, *while unclean,* came within the sweep of the Apostle's damnatory proposition. But the man who is unclean to-day may, by the mercy of God, be clean hereafter. The proposition itself is true universally, true for ever; but not till the Books are opened shall we dare to say that it is true of any person in particular.

No one has any difficulty in perceiving that such limitations as these are as natural as they are necessary in the "damnatory clauses" of Christian morality. Why, then, should they be deemed evasive or non-natural when applied to the " damnatory clauses " of the Athanasian Creed ? If I may say, without offence, that immorality excludes from the kingdom of God, why should it be considered uncharitable to say that heresy also excludes from the kingdom of God ? If wilful resistance to the will of God as revealed in His moral law puts the rebel in jeopardy of everlasting ruin, what ground is there for supposing that we may deprave with impunity the revelation which He has graciously made to us of His eternal nature ?

I can declare therefore, without the slightest shock to my feelings of benevolence, that an Arian or Sabellian "shall perish everlastingly;" but I decline peremptorily to express any opinion whatever on the final destiny of either Arius or Sabellius individually. To do so would be a presumptuous and uncharitable exercise of private judgment utterly unsanctioned either by the Church or Holy Scripture. I find it hard to fathom the mysteries of my own being and to forecast its future; and shall I presume to sit in judgment on the soul of a fellow sinner and pronounce sentence of everlasting perdition upon it ? Certainly I dare not; and, what is more, the Church of God, "pillar and ground of the truth" though she be, has never presumed to do so in her collective capacity, much less encouraged any of her children to do it. Arius depraved the faith of Christendom; and, in vindication of that faith and of the numberless blessings of which it is the guardian, Arius was justly condemned. But **where is Arius now?** And in what relation does he stand to that Lord whose Godhead he blasphemed on earth? Have the scales fallen from his eyes, and does he see the truth at last? Were there any extenuating circumstances in his case which the eye of man could not detect, but for which **He who** " knoweth all things," and " willeth not the death of a sinner," made due allowance? These are questions which **I** cannot answer, and into which I have no warrant to pry. I leave the solution where the Church has left it—in the hands of an all-wise, all-merciful Saviour. **All I** presume to say is that a heretic, as such, shall not inherit the kingdom of God; that no one who wilfully rejects the truth can, during his persistence in error, be in a state of salvation. If Arius is not now in the outer darkness, if he has been at last made " meet for the inheritance of the saints in light," he is no longer an Arian; and it is of the Arian, **the** heretic, the wilful corrupter of the faith, that the Church predicates everlasting perdition, not of the individual soul who bore the name of Arius, and who, for aught I know, may have long since repented of the errors which he taught on earth. This is an answer to those who say that the Athanasian Creed damns Milton to everlasting perdition, because Milton was an Arian. But was he an Arian wilfully and deliberately? That **is to** say, was **the** truth placed before him in such a way that he had no valid excuse for rejecting it? And even then was his rejection of it so persistent and habitual as to deprave his character beyond the possibility of recovery? We must be in a position to affirm all this of Milton, or any other heretic, before we can say that he "shall perish everlastingly."

But this explanation is said to be a mere evasion, and, in fact, a simple explaining away of the "damnatory clauses" of the Athanasian Creed. On the contrary, it is a mere truism in morals, and is at least as old as Aristotle, who lays down in the third Book of his Ethics the very principles of the explanatory note suggested by the Oxford Theological Professors. He draws a fundamental distinction between a wrong act done *in ignorance,* and one done *because of ignorance.* The latter, he says, excuses from all blame; the former does not, but may, on the contrary, aggravate the offence. "There seems to be a farther difference between acting because of ignorance, and doing a thing in ignorance. Common opinion pronounces that the drunken or the angry man does not act because of ignorance, but in consequence of drunkenness or anger, and yet that he does not act wittingly, but in ignorance. Undoubtedly every depraved man is in ignorance of what he ought to do, and of that from which he ought to refrain; and it is in consequence of this error that men become unjust and altogether bad. But the term involuntary is not meant to cover ignorance of man's true interest. Ignorance which affects moral choice, and ignorance of the universal, are the causes, not of involuntary action, but of wickedness; and it is precisely for this ignorance that wicked men are blamed. The ignorance which causes involuntary action is ignorance of particulars, by which I mean the circumstances and the objects of actions. With regard to these particulars, pity and pardon may be proper; for the man who acts in ignorance of some particular is an involuntary agent." *

"The connection of this somewhat compressed passage," says Sir Alexander Grant, "is as follows. An act is involuntary when caused by ignorance. But ignorance cannot be said to be the cause of an act if the individual be himself the cause of the ignorance. In that case ignorance rather accompanies the act (ἀγνοῶν πράττει) than causes it (δι' ἄγνοιαν πράττει). We see this (1) in instances of temporary oblivion, as from anger or wine; (2) in those of a standing moral **ignorance**, or oblivion (εἴ τις ἀγνοεῖ τὸ συμφέρον—ἡ ἐν τῇ προαιρέσει ἄγνοια—ἡ καθόλου ἄγνοια). The only ignorance, then, which is purely external to the agent, so as to take away from him the responsibility of **the** act, is some chance mistake with regard to the particular facts of the case . . . . . Aristotle strictly confines ignorance, as a cause of involuntary action, and therefore as

* 'Nicom. Eth.,' b. iii., c. i., 14–16.

excusing from blame, to mistakes about particulars. Before proceeding to this particular ignorance, he separates from it that kind of ignorance which is faulty, because caused by the agent himself. Of this there are two kinds—the temporary, as, for instance, that caused by intoxication; and the permanent, such as that caused by any vicious habit."*

Aristotle gives the following illustrations of many acts done *because of ignorance,* and therefore excusable. Æschylus, being summoned before the Areopagus on the charge of having revealed the Mysteries, pleaded that he had never himself been initiated, and therefore was not aware that the Mysteries which he had put into one of his Plays corresponded with the real Mysteries. He had therefore sinned *because of ignorance.* Again, there may be a mistake about the thing

---

* 'The Ethics of Aristotle,' illustrated with Essays and Notes. By Sir Alexander Grant, Bart., ii., p. 11.

Cf. Michelet's Commentary *in loc.* δι' ἄγνοιαν πράττειν.) Est ignorantia rerum singularium, quæ cum extra nos et a nobis sint alienæ, si a nobis ignorantur, venia dari potest et impunitas. Ejusmodi ignorantia est causa extranea, vel instrumentum externum quodammodo et a voluntate nostra alienum, etsi in nobis. Quare commode Noster dicit δι' ἄγνοιαν, tanquam ejusmodi facta non per eum, qui agat, sed ipsam per ignorantiam fiant. Sed ἀγνοοῦντα ποιεῖν: *ignorantem quæ ignorare non debemus* (ut officia, bonum) *agere.* Quid sit bonum et justum rectumque nescire est malæ voluntatis; et ejusmodi ignorantia non est extraneum aliquid a voluntate nostra alienum, sed principium internum et qualitas ejus ipsius qui agit. Occurrit idem discrimen in principio jurisperitorum: *Ignorantia juris nocet; ignorantia facti non nocet.*

or person made the object of the action; Merope, for example, **did not know it was her** own son she was killing. Or one **may make a** mistake in respect to an instrument, such as fancying that one's spear had a button on it. **Or the purpose or** tendency of the act might be good, as **one wishing to save** life might, through some misadventure, **kill.** Or one might strike harder than one wished, and **so destroy** life.

The difference, therefore, between sinning *because of ignorance* and sinning *in ignorance* may be stated briefly thus: The first is strictly an act for which no other ultimate cause but ignorance can be assigned. The second will be found to arise from some other ultimate cause, as when a man kills another in a fit of drunkenness. He was unconscious of what he was doing at the time; but he is responsible nevertheless, if he was the cause of his own drunkenness—that is, if he became drunk voluntarily. A man is responsible for every act which is the result of any moral or mental condition which he might have avoided.

Let us apply these considerations to the case before us. A man is in formal heresy, and therefore culpable, when he wilfully rejects the truth. But this is a state **of** mind which **the Dean of** Westminster cannot conceive possible. "**It may be safely** affirmed," he says, "**that, in the only** sense **in which** these **words** can have **any** meaning, no one ever **did** or ever can 'wilfully reject the Catholic faith.'"* With equal plausibility Socrates maintained that no one could be wilfully vicious. And undoubtedly that opinion has an element of truth in it; for "if a perfectly clear intellectual conviction of the goodness of the end and of the necessity of **the** means is present to a man he cannot act otherwise than right." † So, too, it may be said that if a man has a perfectly clear intellectual apprehension of the truth, and an equally clear conviction of the necessity of **em**bracing it, it is morally impossible that he should reject it. But, in both cases, the man may have incapacitated himself for this clear apprehension and conviction by a previous course of misconduct; and therefore he is guilty of wilfully rejecting virtue or truth, though at the moment of rejection his vision of either may be obscure and distorted. For let it be remembered that the intellect, **no** less than the feelings and affections, is capable of contracting bad habits, which need not, however, at all interfere with the soundness and acuteness of it in general, though it may corrupt and disable the judgment upon particular subjects. But who can say of any heretic in particular that his rejection of the truth is of that fatal kind which excludes hope, because **it** denotes an incorrigible perversion of the moral and intellectual faculties? "This is life eternal," says our

---

* 'The Athanasian Creed,' pp. 94, 95.
† Sir A. Grant's 'Essays on Aristotle,' p. 125.

blessed Lord, "that they might know Thee, the only true God, and Jesus Christ whom Thou hast sent." Now if this is true, if life eternal consists in the knowledge of the Trinity in Unity and of the Incarnation, surely he who deliberately rejects these verities puts himself outside the pale of salvation. And by a deliberate rejection I mean a rejection which might have been avoided if the man had made use of his opportunities. An intelligent consent of the will is of the essence of any act of sin whether in the sphere of faith or in that of morals. Heathens, therefore, and in fact all who have never had the Catholic Faith placed before them in such a way that they had no valid excuse for rejecting it, are not touched by the "damnatory clauses" at all. The "damnatory clauses" apply to sinners only, and a sinner is a person who knowingly does wrong, and a man knowingly does wrong not merely who is conscious of wrong-doing in the moment of transgression, but who has reduced himself to a state of moral obliquity which impairs his vision of what is right.

This seems to me such an elementary principle in morals that I find it hard to realize the state of mind of those who denounce it as an evasion. Dr. Swainson is passionate in his repudiation of the plea of "invincible ignorance," or "invincible prejudice." Very good. But how then does he explain our Lord's words, "The time cometh that whosoever killeth you will think that he doeth God service"? What is the state of mind here indicated but one of "invincible prejudice," and therefore pardonable? So, at least, thought a greater authority than Dr. Swainson—one who describes himself as having been before his conversion, "a blasphemer and a persecutor, and a man of overbearing insolence; but I obtained mercy *because I did it ignorantly in unbelief.*" So invincible was the prejudice, that it required "a light from heaven, above the brightness of the sun," to dispel it. Notwithstanding the high authority of Dr. Swainson, then, I am inclined to think that the greatest of heathen philosophers and the most philosophic of inspired Apostles are safer guides to follow than he, and I shall accordingly still continue to believe that "involuntary ignorance or invincible prejudice" is a valid plea in cases of unbelief.

The Dean of Westminster insists, with almost passionate vehemence, that the whole Eastern Church, and divines like Bull and Pearson, are "doomed to everlasting perdition" by the Athanasian Creed: the former for denying that the Holy Ghost proceeds from the Son as well as from the Father, the latter for teaching the doctrine of the Son's subordination to the Father "even as to Divinity." It is impossible to know the Dean of Westminster, even slightly, without feeling some pain at the thought of being in opposition to one so genial and kind-hearted. But he is the last man in England who would think of deprecating adverse criticism on that score. He is very frank in the expression of his own opinions, and I am sure that he will appreciate the most unreserved frankness on the part of those who differ from him, as I do most sincerely, on this question. He will not be offended, then, if I take the liberty of expressing my humble opinion that his strong feeling against the Athanasian Creed has in some degree made him theologically colour-blind in all that relates to this controversy. How is it possible otherwise to explain his reiterated assertion that the Eastern Church and all who think with Bull and Pearson are "doomed to everlasting perdition" by those who believe the Athanasian Creed? If the Dean's view is correct, not only is the whole Eastern Church "doomed to everlasting perdition," but the whole Western Church as well; nay, the author of the Creed has doomed himself to the fate of Bull and Pearson, for he teaches precisely the same doctrine of subordination which is taught by these two distinguished divines, and which is, in fact, one of the truisms of Catholic theology. The doctrine is thus stated by Pearson :—

"The third assertion, next to be demonstrated, is that the Divine essence which Christ had as the Word, before He was conceived by the Virgin Mary, He had not of Himself, but by communication from God the

Father. **For this is not to** be denied, that there can be but one essence properly Divine, and so but one God of infinite wisdom, power, and majesty; that there can **be** but one person originally of Himself subsisting in that infinite Being, because a plurality of more persons so subsisting would necessarily **infer a** multiplicity of Gods; that the **Father of our Lord Jesus Christ is** originally **God, as not** receiving His eternal being from **any** other. Wherefore **it necessarily followeth** that **Jesus** Christ, who **is** certainly **not the** Father, cannot **be a** person subsisting **in** the Divine nature originally of Himself; and consequently, being we have already proved that He is truly and properly the Eternal God, He must be understood to have the Godhead communicated to Him by the **Father, who is** not only eternally, but originally, God. *All things whatsoever the Father hath are mine*, saith **Christ**; because in Him is the fulness of the Godhead, and more than that the Father cannot have; but yet in that *perfect and absolute equality* there is, notwithstanding, this disparity, that the Father **hath the** Godhead not from the Son, nor any other, whereas the Son hath it from the Father: Christ **is** the true God and eternal life; but that He is so is from the Father: *for as the Father hath life in Himself,* **so** *hath He given to the Son to have* **life** *in Himself,* not by participation, but by communication. It is true our Saviour was so in the form of God that He thought it no robbery to be equal

with God; but when the Jews sought to kill Him
because He *made Himself equal with God*, He answered
them, *Verily, verily,* **I** *say unto you, the Son can do
nothing of Himself, but what He seeth the Father do* : by
that connection of **His** operations showing the reception of His essence ; and by the acknowledgment of
His power professing His substance from the Father.
From whence He who was equal, even in that equality
confesseth a priority, saying, *the Father is greater than*
I : the Son *equal in respect of His nature,* the Father
greater in reference to the communication of the God-
head. *I know Him,* saith Christ, *for I am from Him.*
And because he is from the Father, therefore He is
called by those of the Nicene Council, in their Creed,
God *of God, Light of Light, very God of very God.*
The Father is God, but not of God ; Light, but not of
Light ; Christ is God, but of God ; Light, but of Light.
There is no difference **or** *inequality in the nature or
essence, because the same in both ;* but the Father of our
Lord Jesus Christ hath that essence of Himself, from
none ; Christ hath the same not of Himself, but from
Him. And being the Divine Nature, as it is absolutely
immaterial and incorporeal, is also indivisible, *Christ
cannot have any part of it only communicated unto Him,
but the whole,* by which he must be acknowledged co-
essential, of the same substance, with the Father ; as
the Council of Nice determined, and the ancient fathers
before them **taught.** Hence appeareth the **truth of**

those words of our Saviour, which raised a second motion in the Jews to stone him; *I and the Father are one*: where the plurality of the verb, and the neutrality of the noun, with the distinction of their persons, speak a perfect identity of their essence. And though Christ say, *the Father is in Me and I in Him;* yet withal he saith, *I came out from the Father;* by the former showing the Divinity of His essence, by the latter the origination of Himself." *

And Hooker:—

" By the gift of eternal generation Christ hath received of the Father one and in number the self-same substance, which the Father hath of Himself unreceived from any other. For every beginning is a father unto that which cometh of it; and every offspring is a son unto that out of which it groweth. Seeing therefore the Father alone is originally that Deity which Christ originally is not (for Christ is God by being of God, light by issuing out of light), it followeth hereupon that whatsoever Christ hath common unto Him with His Heavenly Father, the same of necessity must be *given* Him, *but naturally and eternally given,* not bestowed by way of benevolence and favour, as the other gifts both are. And therefore when the Fathers give out for a rule, that whatsoever Christ is said in Scripture to have received, the same we ought to apply only to the manhood of Christ; their assertion is true of all

* 'On the Creed,' i., pp. 170-2.

things which Christ hath received by grace, but to that which he hath received of the Father by *eternal nativity or birth* it reacheth not."*

With this agrees the passage quoted by the Dean of Westminster from Bishop Bull:—

"The Catholic Doctors, both **before** and after **the Nicene Council, are** unanimous in declaring that the Father is greater than the Son, even as to Divinity— *i. e. not in virtue of any essential perfection,* but alone in **what** may be called authority—that is, in point of origin, since **the Son is** from the Father, not the Father **from the Son.**"

If the question were one in which the Dean's feelings were not so strongly enlisted **as they** are in this, it could hardly have escaped him that **the** words which I have marked by italics, in the quotation from Bishop Bull, are a complete answer to his objection; for they show distinctly that the subordination of the Son to the Father, which Bishop Bull, in common with the **whole Catholic** Church, teaches, is not at all **incon-**

---

* 'Eccles. Polity,' b. v., liv., 2. It is evident that Hooker had no idea **that in** teaching the doctrine of the Son's subordination he was making himself amenable to the "damnatory clauses" of the Athanasian **Creed; for he** asks, "Is there in that confession of faith (*i. e.* Athanasian Creed) anything which doth not at all times edify and instruct the **attentive** hearer? Or is our faith in the blessed Trinity a matter needless to be so oftentimes mentioned and opened in the principal part of that duty which we owe to God, our public prayer?"—B. v., ch. xlii., 12.

sistent with the assertion of the Athanasian Creed, that " in this Trinity none is afore or after other, none is greater or less than another; but the whole Three Persons are co-eternal together and co-equal." " In nature or any essential perfection" "none is afore or after other, none is greater or less than another." But in point of order the Father is " the fount of Deity " ($\pi\eta\gamma\acute{\eta}$ $\theta\epsilon\acute{o}\tau\eta\tau o\varsigma$), and the Son and Holy Spirit derive their divinity from Him, as the stream is derived from the fountain and the ray from the sun. In this respect, and in this only, the Father may be called greater than the Son and Holy Spirit. But it is not in this respect that the Athanasian Creed asserts their perfect equality; for it says, immediately before, that " the Father is made of none; neither created nor begotten. The Son is of the Father alone; not made nor created, but begotten." Here is the very subordination on which Bishop Bull insists. " The Father is made of none," but the Son is of the Father, not in time, but in respect to derivation; for, of course, the relations of the Persons of the Trinity to each other are eternal relations. In our finite experience a son is posterior to his father in point of time. But notions derived from temporal relations are obviously inapplicable to a state of existence which is altogether independent of space and time. Both the Apostles' Creed and the Nicene, as well as Holy Scripture, plainly intimate that Fatherhood is an essential attribute of the first Person of the Blessed Trinity. As He was always Almighty, so He was always the Father of His only-begotten Son, who is therefore rightly called "the eternal Son" "begotten of His Father before all worlds." And thus the relation of God the Father to His coeval Son does not imply priority of existence, or inequality of power or glory, but simply a difference of order.

I know how very difficult it is to express these things in language which shall be accurate and intelligible at the same time. "No tongue, how perfect soever it may appear, is a complete and perfect instrument of human thought. From its very conditions every language must be imperfect. The human memory can only compass a limited complement of words; but the data of sense, and still more the combinations of the understanding, are wholly unlimited in number. No language can, therefore, be adequate to the ends for which it exists; all are imperfect."[*] If human language is thus imperfect when it deals with the ordinary conceptions of the human mind, how much more incompetent must it be to give articulate expression to mysteries which the intellect of man cannot grasp? The truths of eternity are far too vast to be capable of being envisaged in the forms of time, and even the profoundest minds, when they make the attempt, are, at best, like Moses in the cleft

[*] Sir W. Hamilton's 'Lectures on Metaphysics and Logic,' iv., p. 143.

of the rock on Horeb, not able to behold the "face," but only the "back parts" of the vision which is graciously vouchsafed to them. "Divine truth," as has been well observed by a divine who is less known than he deserves to be, "hath its humiliation and exanition, as well as its exaltation. Divine truth becomes many times in Scripture incarnate, debasing itself to assume our rude conceptions, that so it might converse more freely with us, and infuse its Divinity in us; God having been pleased herein to manifest Himself not more jealous of His own glory than He is (as I may say) zealous of our good. *Nos non habemus aures sicut Deus habet linguam.* If He should speak in the language of eternity, who could understand Him, or interpret His meaning? Or if he should have declared His truth to us only in the way of the purest abstraction that human souls are capable of, how should then the more rude and illiterate sort of men have been able to apprehend it? Truth is content, when it comes into the world, to wear our mantles, to learn our language, to conform itself, as it were, to our dress and fashions."* But our dress never fits it, and can at best do no more than give a faint outline of its form. Yet the dress is necessary, for without it we should have no idea at all of those great realities which lie behind this shifting scene of fleeting phe-

* 'Select Discourses' of John Smith, the Cambridge Platonist, p. 173.

nomena. God the Father and His Eternal Son are not related to each other as a human father and son are related; and yet the human relationship may be the nearest approach to the truth of which our feeble minds are capable.

I shall continue to use the Athanasian Creed, then, without any fear that I am thereby consigning "to everlasting perdition" Bull and Pearson, who are in full agreement with the Church universal in teaching the perfect equality of the Father and the Son in all essential attributes, save only that which is peculiar to each, namely, Fatherhood and Sonship. In the Divine Essence, which is common to the Three Persons, there is no inequality; but in their interior relation to each other there is a subordination of order.

Equally untenable, I venture to think, is Dean Stanley's assertion that the whole Eastern Church is doomed to "perish everlastingly," if the Athanasian Creed is true. The difference between the Eastern Church and the West on the vexed question of the *Filioque* is clearly a difference of statement, not of doctrine. It all turns on the meaning of the word "procession," which the Easterns use in one sense, and the Westerns in another; so that what the former deny is not what the latter affirm, and *vice versâ*. The phrase is manifestly equivocal, as the logicians say, and there are senses in which the Greeks would accept it without hesitation. They hold, as do the Westerns, that the Holy Ghost proceeds from the Father alone with respect to that Personality which is the *cause* of the Trinity; but they admit that He proceeds from the Son also in respect of that common Essence of Deity, which is numerically one in the Three Persons, but which the Holy Spirit receives from the Person of the Father as the cause.

Again, it may be said that the Holy Ghost "proceedeth from the Father and the Son" in this way: from the Father alone in respect of His own Personality, or origin* as a Person, but from the Son also in respect of His Essence considered apart—I mean apart by an abstraction of human thought, not as a theological reality.

A third sense in which the Greeks would admit that the Holy Ghost proceeds from the Father and the Son is in respect of temporal mission. The Son *sends* the Holy Ghost *from* the Father, and therefore the procession is from both the Father and the Son, though in different senses.

In short, what the Greeks are anxious to protect is the *Monarchia* of the Trinity, and they fear that by admitting the *Filioque* they would sanction the notion

---

* It is scarcely necessary to explain that the word "origin" is used here, and elsewhere in this connection, as indicating derivation, not beginning of existence; as a flame is the origin of the light which it diffuses without being therefore anterior to the light, or as heat derives its origin from fire without necessarily coming after it in the order of time.

that there are two ἀρχαί in the Trinity, or that there was something besides the Three distinct Persons and the one Common Essence, namely, some peculiar Essence belonging to the Father and the Son apart from the Holy Spirit. These are two errors which the whole of the Western Church would repudiate as heartily as the Eastern; and if both sides would only act on Dr. Newman's advice, and define instead of disputing, the controversy about the *Filioque* would speedily come to a peaceful end.

The Greek Church, therefore, would not be touched by the " damnatory clauses " of the Athanasian Creed, even if we were to transfer to it the *Filioque* of the Nicene Creed, for it would still remain a question whether the doctrine affirmed in the one case was denied in the other. But, as a matter of fact, the *Filioque* does not exist in the Athanasian Creed. The words of the Creed are, " The Holy Ghost is of (*a* not *ex*) the Father and of the Son; neither made, nor created, nor begotten, but proceeding." No Greek doctrine comes in collision with this statement. Even Mr. Ffoulkes[*] admits that "it is literally moderation itself. Few advocates of the Latin doctrine would have been content to stop where it stops; few Greeks . . . would have declined going as far. The Holy Ghost is described as 'of the Father and of the Son,' first—the preposition used being *a*, not *ex*: and then

---

[*] 'On the Athanasian Creed,' p. 263.

'neither made, nor created, nor begotten, but proceeding.' The copula, rigidly supplied in the two previous verses, is altogether wanting in this. The words may imply, but they certainly stop short of asserting, that 'the Holy Ghost *proceeds* from the Son' in the Latin sense, '*ex* Patre Filioque procedit.'" And yet Mr. Ffoulkes has written a book of 374 pages to prove that this very Creed, which "is moderation itself," and to which "few Greeks" would object, was wickedly and fraudulently imposed on Christendom by Charlemagne and two of the ablest divines and best men of their age, for no other purpose than to cause a schism between East and West! But I am not concerned with Mr. Ffoulkes's historical vagaries here. His own book contains abundant materials for its own refutation, and his wild theory has already been sufficiently disposed of by competent scholars. What I wish to point out is that a writer, whose antipathy to the Athanasian Creed amounts to a kind of craze, is obliged to confess that its "damnatory clauses" do not touch the Greek Church at all. I do trust, therefore, that we shall hear no more of the Greek Church being "doomed to everlasting perdition" by those who advocate the retention of the Athanasian Creed in its present position.

But, after all, what is meant by "perishing everlastingly"? The late Mr. Charles Buxton objected, as one of the Ritual Commissioners, to the Athanasian Creed, because, among other things, " it commits the Church of England to the doctrine, long since exploded, that error is a crime punishable with horrible torments." Now I am not prepared to deny that error, if wilful, does entail " horrible torments." It is often so in this life, and I see no reason why it should be otherwise in the world unseen. But, on the other hand, wilful sin, whether in faith or morals, brings its own punishment. God is only indirectly the author of the sinner's torments by having given him a constitution which, in virtue of free will, is capable of being ruined; and in that ruin lies the misery of the lost. But it is easy to see that what Mr. Buxton had before his mind was the image of a vengeful Miltonic Deity, " hurling headlong . . . . down to bottomless perdition" the erring victims of His implacable wrath.

This, I need hardly say, is not the doctrine of the Church, however individual writers may here and there have caricatured her teaching. When the Pharisees asked our Lord, " When the kingdom of God should come?" He answered, " The kingdom of God is *within you*." With equal truth it may be said that the kingdom of Satan is also *within us*. Each man has within himself, during the period of his probation, the elements of his own final condition. His character is developed from within, and outward circumstances are but the passive materials on which it feeds. They are necessary to its growth, but they do not determine the direction in which it shall grow; that is the province of man's free will, which makes him master of his circumstances, not their slave. In this respect man differs essentially from all else that lives upon this earth. He possesses a conscious, self-determining power, and can shape all external influences after the fashion of the governing principle which rules his conduct from within. In one sense, indeed, all organic existences may be said to have a self-determining power. Every form of created life in the universe is built upon a certain type, and aspires, consciously or unconsciously, to some ideal as the final cause of its existence; and any life, from an acorn to an Archangel, which fails to realize the end of its being, may truly be said to "perish everlastingly." It happened to me, not long ago, to wander through a forest by the sea, in which all the trees were misshapen and stunted. They had been exposed to the withering blasts of an eastern ocean during their period of growth, and so they were not able to reach the perfection of which their nature was potentially capable. They had passed their probation, they had arrived at maturity, and had no longer any possibility of amendment. The tempest might break or root them up; but no force of man or nature could ever again change their shapes without destroying them. They "perished everlastingly."

Have we not here a parable of human life? Man's soul, like a tree, or like the body which clothes it, has its period of growth, and tends to a state of unchanging fixedness. It is as true of him as of the trees of the forest that the influences of a comparatively short period determine the character of a period indefinitely long. Exposure to a demoralizing set of influences for a given time may fix the character so irrevocably in a wrong groove that, in Scriptural language, it is "impossible to renew it again unto repentance." And, on the other hand, perseverance in the right way will, in due time, impress upon the human will such a character of strict conformity to God's will, that it can no longer be tempted to evil; "sin will no more have dominion over it," and a fall will be impossible.

But the analogy of the vegetable kingdom does not carry us very far. There is a vital difference between the development of a tree and that of human character. For the tree is at the mercy of surrounding circumstances; it cannot move out of its place or protect itself against the influences of the eastern breeze. But man can rise superior to circumstances. He can "work out his own salvation," and can turn even his temptations into blessings. No combination of circumstances, however hostile, can injure his true self without the concurrence of his own free and presiding will. He is thus the author of his own final destiny, whatever that destiny may be. God damns none of His creatures to everlasting perdition. He shuts the door of heaven against no one who has not previously closed it on himself. In making man capable of everlasting bliss He has necessarily made him capable of everlasting perdition. God Almighty Himself, with reverence be it said, could not create a being who should be capable of virtue without leaving him, at the same time, capable of sin. For virtue implies a free will, and a free will implies the power of choice, and liberty of choice implies the possibility of making a wrong choice, and a wrong choice, confirmed into a habit, may result in such a moral paralysis as shall make recovery impossible. The man who has thus reduced himself to a state of "incorrigibility," to use Aristotle's phrase, "finds no place of repentance," not because God refuses to be gracious, but because the perverted will no longer possesses the power of making a right choice.

Is it not strange that, in an age when the fixity and invariability of Nature's laws is preached as almost a new Gospel, men should forget—and scientific men are among the chief offenders—that human character, too, has its laws, and that its laws are—what the mechanical laws of the Universe are not—in a certain degree independent of the will of God? There is no reason at all in the nature of things why we should confidently expect the continuance of the present order of things in the natural world. Apart from faith in God, our only ground of confidence is in the subjective impression made on our imaginations by the immemorial uniformity of the laws which govern our system. It would not contradict any of the laws of thought if we were told that there were other systems similar to ours, but governed by an entirely different system of laws. But we cannot conceive the possibility of a virtuous being who never had any freedom of choice, or of a really free will which could not rebel against its Maker for ever and make itself miserable for ever in consequence.

Undoubtedly God might have created intelligent beings who should obey Him unceasingly under a law of mechanical necessity. But He could not have created beings capable of yielding Him a moral service without bestowing on them the awful gift of a free will—the power to do or to forbear. The lower creation, through all its ranks, obeys its Maker's will. "He hath given them a law which shall not be broken," and therefore "they continue this day according to Thine ordinance, for all things serve Thee." They have no power of doing otherwise; they cannot choose but to obey. Nor are the lower animals an exception. Their movements may appear more free than the motions of the heavenly bodies or the changes of the vegetable kingdom. But, after all, they have only the semblance of a free will, not the reality. They have no reasoning faculty properly so called; they cannot analyze or generalize. They can remember in a dull passive way, but they cannot recollect; they cannot gather up the impressions of the past and make them available for the purposes of the future. In fact, they have neither future nor past—no lively memories or bitter regrets connected with the one, no hopes or prospects connected with the other. They do not contemplate themselves at all. They live in the present, and have no thought beyond the passing hour. Man can impress his will upon them in a measure. He may improve them in breed, as flowers and trees may be improved by cultivation. But there is a certain point beyond which he cannot train them; for they have no real freedom, no self-determining power; and they are consequently incapable of progress. Each of them begins life as if the first of its race, deriving no advantage from the experience of its predecessors, and leaving no legacy of acquirements to those which follow. They "have no understanding," as the Psalmist says, and are therefore "held with bit and bridle."

But man is the subject of a moral Government whose laws he may transgress if he will. His loving Father strives to attract him. He places before him life and death, and bids him choose life, and gives him grace sufficient for his needs. He does everything, in fact, to win him, short of compulsion, because compulsion would be incompatible with freedom, and therefore with virtue. "I will inform thee and teach thee in the way wherein thou shalt go, and *I will guide thee with mine eye,*" not "with bit and bridle," like the lower animals "which have no understanding." If, however, we persist in being like the horse and mule, there is no help for it; God leads us only *with His eye;* there is no bit and bridle to restrain us; our wills are free and we may go to ruin.

True freedom, however, does not mean the power to choose good *or* evil. So long as the will is capable of vacillating between right and wrong it is not really free any more than a limb is free which is shaken by paralysis. A man is truly free when his will is only attracted by legitimate objects, and "sin has no more dominion over him." God could, of course, have created intelligent beings unalterably fixed on the side of right from the moment of their creation. But a will which never had a choice would not be free—would not, in fact, be will at all. It is necessary to our conception of a created free will that it should start with the power of choosing one of two opposite courses—good or evil—and then become, by persevering efforts, so self-determined in the right line as to lose all possibility of doing wrong. When the will has reached this stage it can no longer be tempted to choose evil. The man acts rightly spontaneously and without effort, and his inability to do wrong does not arise from any extraneous restraint, but from the fact that he is become "a law unto himself." He has disciplined his will into perfect and habitual conformity with the will of God, and it is therefore as impossible any longer to tempt him from the right way as it is to "renew again unto repentance" the incorrigibly selfish. To such a soul God's service is no longer irksome or difficult; it is "perfect freedom," as one of our collects beautifully expresses it; just as God Himself is the freest of all beings, though it would be blasphemy to suppose Him capable of doing wrong. Liability to error is, on the face of it, a proof that the will is, so far, imperfect, not that it is in a state of healthy freedom.

I may seem to be insisting unnecessarily on what every well-educated person will at once recognize as a truism in morals. It *is* a truism; but it is very hard to get a certain class of minds to grasp even a truism when it cuts across their prejudices. There is, for instance, a violent article against the Athanasian Creed in the April number of the 'Contemporary Review,' which denies peremptorily the truisms on which I have been insisting above, and uses them, in fact, as one of the chief arguments against the Athanasian Creed. The writer, who signs himself "Anglicanus," animadverts on "a common argument, recently adduced by the late Archbishop Longley, to the effect that the same word 'eternal' (αἰώνιος) is applied to both states of the departed, and that if heaven is 'everlasting,' so must the other state be." "The answer," "Anglicanus" thinks, "is not very clear or satisfying, if we assume that the good are fixed in heaven for ever by an immutable decree, and that falling from it is an impossibility. The very essence of spirit is freedom, and we cannot be secured an 'eternal heaven' by any sort of mechanical fixation. An eternity of either virtue or blessedness cannot be guaranteed to us—it must depend on ourselves. Are we not told of certain 'angels who kept not their first estate, but left their own habitation'? A fall may be improbable, but it cannot be impossible so long as mind and free choice remain."

This passage reveals a great deal. It shows, among other things, that much of the feeling against the Athanasian Creed is really based on the grossest ignorance of the very rudiments of moral science. Here is a gentleman, evidently of education, who comes forward to enlighten the public on the Athanasian Creed, and he delivers himself of an Essay which proves to demonstration that of theology and Christian ethics he simply knows nothing. With the innocent ingenuousness of ignorance he coolly propounds a doctrine which strikes at the very foundations of both theology and morality. For if "the very essence of spirit is freedom," and freedom means an endless liability to sin, we have no real security against the final triumph of evil over Almighty God Himself. Evil may eventually become good, and good evil. The "great gulf fixed" between the abode of the lost and that of the blessed may at length be passed, and the inhabitants of heaven may exchange places with the denizens of hell. Surely to state such a theory is to refute it; yet it is on a par with the reasoning of the whole Essay. What is to be thought of a reasoner who actually thinks that the doctrine of eternal perdition is confuted by the article of the Creed which declares "the forgiveness of sins"? "Observe," he says, "to what puny and pitiful dimensions this glorious clause of the Creed has been reduced by the progress of dogmatic development. 'Forgiveness of sins' is limited—to this world and to this life! We must have our pardon sealed in heaven before we go hence and be no more seen. Forgiveness of sin, then, is a thing of time and space; it is a geographical consideration. It is accorded only within the narrowest limits. That which results from, and is an expression of, the unchanging mind and nature of God is a thing 'subject to all the skyey influences.' The temperature changes; there is a sudden access of frost or cold, the man dies; from that moment the hitherto relenting Deity, who wooed the sinner with the sweetest tones of mercy and the fullest assurance of pardon, is changed on the sudden, and is henceforth and for ever to him as deaf as the wind, as inexorable as the roaring sea. The Eternal is subject to Time! the Omnipotent is limited to a poor corner of space! These considerations are enough to disprove the whole doctrine, and show it to be but a fable. According to the current doctrine, what is true of the Almighty to-day may be false to-morrow. He is merciful one day, inexorable the next." And then " Anglicanus " thinks that such prayers as the following :—" O God, whose *nature and property is ever to have mercy and to forgive*";* or such Psalms as speak of God's mercy " *enduring for ever*,"* —are plainly inconsistent with the notion of any creature perishing everlastingly. And he denounces the Athanasian Creed accordingly. It teaches " a doctrine worthy only of the priests of Moloch!" and " an inward revulsion seizes the minds of all who hear it; one's gorge rises at the very name of it."

It would have been more modest on the part of " Anglicanus " not to have assumed that all other gorges are in the same state of morbid irritation as his own. What authority has he for asserting that " an inward revulsion seizes the minds of all who hear " the Athanasian Creed? The multitude of petitions lately presented to Convocation in its favour is a curious commentary on the wild declamation of " Anglicanus." Who he is I know not, except that he is not the distinguished ecclesiastic who sometimes assumes the *nom de plume* of " Anglicanus." But whoever the

* The italics are not mine.

"Anglicanus" of the 'Contemporary Review' is, he has evidently yet to learn the rudiments of Christian ethics. As a matter of fact, our Lord has said that there is a sin which is "*never forgiven*, neither in this world, nor in that which is to come." But I do not dwell on this. Let it suffice to point out that "Anglicanus" misses the whole point of the question which he has discussed with an intemperate zeal which certainly is "not according to knowledge." The question is not whether God's "mercy endureth for ever," but whether the sinner will for ever remain amenable to its influence. God, of course, remains ever the same —"the same yesterday, to-day, and for ever." His love is not stinted by the sins of His creatures, nor changed to hate by the fact of their death. But, on the other hand, Divine love, in its essence and manifestation, implies freedom in those with whom it has to do. Its power is such that wherever there is the least germ of moral life it can develop it. But is it not possible for man to destroy this germ so as to retain no elements within him upon which the love of God can act? Does not the mystery of human freedom imply the possibility, at least, that some may be eternally lost? Is it not a fact of experience that men do actually resist the holiest strivings of Divine love on earth? And if on earth, why not in the world unseen? If the human will remain essentially the same (and if it do not, the man is no longer the same person), why should it be impossible for it to continue its resistance to Divine grace *ad infinitum*? Either it can do so, or one of the essential elements in man's constitution is destroyed, and he ceases, in fact, to be man. What use is forgiveness to the impenitent prodigal who still prefers the " riotous living " in the " far country " to the feast in his Father's house? The sore distress which softens one heart may harden another. If one prodigal is constrained to cry, " I will arise and go to my Father," another may assert his freedom by persevering in his evil ways. Of what avail is it, then, that God's " nature and property is ever **to have** mercy to forgive," if the sinner remains still obdurate **in** his sin? Can he do so? If not, his liberty is a myth, and he is not a responsible being; from which it follows that, as he is not capable of sin, he is not susceptible of forgiveness. If, on the contrary, he can offer an endless resistance to the Divine will, he may make himself the victim of a never-ending misery—that is to say, he can " perish everlastingly." But in that case, he is himself, and not God, the sole cause of his own ruin.

This doctrine appears to me very simple and reasonable, and **not** hard to be understood; and **I** am therefore all the more surprised that **a** periodical usually so dispassionate and acute as the ' Westminster Review' should have offered to its readers the following caricature of the doctrine of the Fall and its consequences:—" God was in the beginning, as **He** is still, omnipotent, omnibenevolent, omniscient, prescient. He said, 'I will create a being whom I shall call man. I could create him, if I so wished, not only perfect, but free from all risk of imperfection to come. But I shall not do this. I shall create him with a faculty for disobeying me, which will be a flaw in him. I know beforehand that he will exercise this faculty, and when he does I will consign him to endless misery and perdition.' "*

I should like to ask the writer of this article whether he believes that man is really free to make a moral choice. If he admits as much, he cannot deny that the Fall of man is a possible consequence of his freedom, and that such a fall may have its consummation in " endless misery and perdition." But to such a doom God " consigns " no one. Certainly He need not have created such a being as man at all. But having created such a being, I should like to know how even " Omniscience," " Omnipotence," and " Omnibenevolence " combined could have prevented the catastrophe, with all its consequences, which is commonly called the Fall. No doubt, God could have created a being " free from all risk of imperfection to come." But such a being would not be man. The quarrel of the 'Westminster Reviewer,' if he would only be logical, is not with the doctrine of the Fall and of endless misery, but with the creation of moral agents at all.

* 'Westminster Review,' April, 1872, p. 382.

Once grant the existence of an intelligent moral being, and all the rest follows, as Bishop Butler has it, " by way of natural consequence." At all events, man, with his liability to sin and capacity of misery, is a fact which Theology has not made, but found; and those who quarrel with the account of the matter which Theology furnishes are bound to give an account of their own, which shall be more in harmony with reason and with facts. Until they have done so, I shall continue to believe that Christian Theology supplies not only the most rational, but the only rational, theory of man's origin and destiny.

But this is by the way, for I am not concerned here with the professed impugners of the Christian Faith, but with those whose repugnance to the Athanasian Creed arises, as I humbly venture to think, from a hasty misunderstanding of its "damnatory clauses." Their error, if I may presume to say so, is twofold : they forget, in the first place, that the "damnatory clauses" cannot possibly apply to any but such as wilfully deprave the Faith, since the conscious consent of the will is essential to any act of sin ;* and, in the second place, they imagine that everlasting perdition means a punishment inflicted arbitrarily from without by an angry God, instead of being, as I believe, the

* "A state or act, that has not its origin in the will, may be calamity, deformity, disease, or mischief; but a sin it cannot be."—Coleridge's 'Aids to Reflection,' p. 215.

natural consequence of inward dispositions on the part of man. "The happiness which good men shall partake is not distinct from their God-like nature. Happiness and holiness are but two several notions of one thing. Hell is rather a nature than a place, and Heaven cannot be so well-defined by anything *without* us as by something within us."* The incorrigible sinner is in hell wherever his local habitation may happen to be, for he carries the undying worm and the unquenchable fire within him. Material flames, if applicable at all to an immaterial being, could add but little to the agony of "a mind diseased." The immaterial part of man is, after all, the real seat of pain, and we know that even in this life a powerful mental emotion will make a man insensible to the pangs of bodily wounds. In the aberration of noble endowments, in the anarchy of a ruined constitution, in the consuming restlessness of matured selfishness—"seeking rest and finding none"—in the remembrance of joys that might have been, but now can be no more,† a soul abandoned to the intolerable tyranny of its own "will-worship" (ἐθελοθρησκεία) will find its surest and

---

* Mr. John Smith's 'Select Discourses.' 'On the Happiness and Nobleness of True Religion.' Edition of 1673. This passage is amplified and marred in subsequent editions.

† ". . . . nessun maggior dolore
　　Che ricordarsi del tempo felice
　　Nella miseria."—Dante, *Inferno*, cant. v. 121.

G

most terrible hell. This view of the self-engendered endless misery of the impenitent sinner is put with remarkable force and clearness by a writer who will not be accused of undue reverence for traditional views of religion. "In the present state," says Channing,* "we find that the mind has an immense power over the body, and, when diseased, often communicates disease to its sympathizing companion. I believe that in the future state the mind will have this power of conforming its outward frame to itself incomparably more than here. We must never forget that, in that world, mind or character is to exert an all-powerful sway ; and accordingly it is rational to believe that the corrupt and deformed mind which wants moral goodness, or a spirit of concord with God and with the Universe, will create for itself as its fit dwelling a deformed body, which will also want concord or harmony with all things around it. Suppose this to exist, and the whole creation which now amuses may become an instrument of suffering, fixing the soul with a more harrowing consciousness on itself. You know that even now, in consequence of certain derangements of the nervous system, the beautiful light gives acute pain, and sounds which once delighted us become shrill and distressing. How often this excessive irritableness of the body has its origin in moral disorders perhaps few of us suspect.

* Works, vol. iv., pp. 164–166.

I apprehend, indeed, that we should be all amazed were we to learn to what extent the body is continually incapacitated for enjoyment, and made susceptible of suffering, by the sins of the heart and life. That delicate part of our organization on which sensibility, pain, and pleasure depend, is, I believe, peculiarly alive to the touch of moral evil. How easily, then, may the mind hereafter frame the future body according to itself, so that, in proportion to its vice, it will receive through its organs and senses impressions of gloom which it will feel to be the natural productions of its own depravity, and which will in this way give a terrible energy to conscience! For myself, I see no need of a local hell for the sinner after death. When I reflect how, in the present world, a guilty mind has power to deform the countenance, to undermine health, to poison pleasure, to darken the fairest scenes of nature, to turn prosperity into a curse, I can easily understand how, in the world to come, sin, working without obstruction according to its own nature, should spread the gloom of a dungeon over the whole creation, and, wherever it goes, should turn the universe into a hell."

This is a terrible commentary on S. Paul's Resurrection doctrine: "To every seed his own body." Every seed has its own specific life, which builds around it an outward organization suited to its peculiar character. The human frame is made up of material particles identical in kind with those which compose the bodies of the brutes that perish, and the difference of organization is in virtue of the different vital principles which energize from within. Man was created in the image of his God; but if he subordinates the spiritual to the animal part of his nature, does it not stand to reason that the development of his character will be in a brutish direction, and that the image of Christ will be changed into that of the sin to which he clung during the period of his probation, and which now clings to him like the poisoned shirt of Nessus? Death does not break the continuity of human life; it merely disengages the man's true self from the restraints and environments of this world, and reveals him just as he is—transformed into the image of his Saviour or into that of the Fiend. Thus viewed old age is very instructive. As the bodily functions decay and the intellectual powers become relaxed, the genuine character of the man begins to show itself, and we behold either the moroseness and peevishness of matured selfishness, no longer kept in check by the artificial restraints of a calculating prudence; or, on the other hand, the glory of the immortal life reflected on silver hairs, and lighting up the countenance with a serene beauty and a benign cheerfulness which are not of this earth.

This is, in fact, the true import of the Greek word (κρίσις) which is sometimes translated "judgment," and sometimes "damnation," in our English Version. It really means a separation or division, and would not be inappropriately translated by its English equivalent, *crisis*. What do we mean by a crisis? Do we not mean the arrival of antagonistic elements at such a pass that a separation is imminent, and one or other must triumph? A fever has reached its crisis when the principle of life and the principle of decay are face to face and one of them is about to obtain the mastery. A debate in Parliament has reached its crisis when the *division* takes place, and the members file off to the right hand and to the left of the presiding judge, each following out to their legitimate results the principles which have ruled his political conduct. And what is the "judgment" (κρίσις) of the Last Day but the crisis of humanity, the final separation of the antagonistic elements of moral good and moral evil? The wheat and the tares grow together till the harvest; the sheep and the goats live together till the Great White Throne is set. And then will take place the irrevocable separation. Humanity will cleave asunder, and every child of Adam will be drawn, by the force of an irresistible attraction, to that sphere of light or darkness for which he has prepared himself here. "Where your treasure is, there will your heart be also." That is a universal law of human nature. The heart cannot be separated from its treasure, and if the treasure is laid up where selfishness reigns supreme the heart cannot choose but follow it. The irreclaimable sinner is dragged to hell by the fierce relentless tyranny of his own unbridled passions. Like attracts like, and as surely as the magnet attracts the needle so surely will hell, the kingdom of supreme selfishness, draw to itself all souls in whom self is the dominant motive. "In order to direct the view aright," says an old writer, "it behooves that the beholder should have made himself congenerous and similar to the object beheld. Never could the eye have beheld the sun had not its essence been soliform—preconfigured to light by a similarity of essence to that of light. Neither can a soul not beautiful within attain to an intuition and enjoyment of beauty." Heaven, so far from attracting, would repel all whose dispositions are not heavenly. The destiny of every human soul at last is to "go to his own place"—to that home, whether of misery or bliss, where its treasures are laid up. And this destiny is sometimes fixed irrevocably, for nations and for individuals, by what men ignorantly call trifles. In the conflict of virtue and vice all may be doubtful up to a certain point; then a crisis is reached when one single act, apparently of slight significance, consolidates a series of previous acts into an unalterable character, and the man or the community is lost for ever. A while ago heaven was possible; now there is the "great gulf fixed" which cannot be passed. Do we not sometimes see shadows of these terrible realities cast athwart this lower world? A nation, a church, a man, is bidden, like Hercules in the fable of Prodicus, to choose, once for all, one of two courses; and a wrong choice having been deliberately made, retreat is found to be impossible; there is "no place of repentance, though sought carefully with tears."

> "Once to every man and nation comes the moment to decide,
> In the strife of truth with falsehood, for the good or evil side.
> Some great cause, God's new Messiah, offering each the bloom or blight,
> Parts the goats upon the left hand and the sheep upon the right;
> And the choice goes by for ever 'twixt that darkness and that light."

But many, probably most, of those who dislike the Athanasian Creed would admit all this in the case of moral offences. They would admit that deliberate violations of the moral law may entail endless misery on the offender.* But they do not seem to see that it is really

---

* The Dean of Westminster seems to deny this. "There are many severe sentences in Scripture," he says; "but there is none which says even of murderers or of hypocrites, '*whosoever* is a murderer, *whosoever* is a hypocrite, *shall without doubt perish everlastingly.*'" Surely this is a hasty assertion. What does the Dean say to the following passages:—

"Whoso hateth his brother is a murderer, and ye know that no murderer hath eternal life abiding in him."—(1 John iii. 15.)

The loss of eternal life is perdition, and it is this perdition which "the disciple whom Jesus loved" predicates of *everyone* who is a murderer even in thought. His assertion is therefore

as reprehensible to reject any part of the contents of Revelation as it is to reject any part of the moral law. They cannot understand that persistence in heresy can have any vital influence on the final condition of one whose moral conduct is, in other respects, irreproachable; and they believe, though they shrink from clothing their thoughts in words, that, after all, it does not very much matter what a man believes, so long as he leads a good and honest life. This view has been equivalent to saying, "whosoever is a murderer shall perish everlastingly."

Again the same Apostle says:—

"The fearful (*i. e.* moral cowards) and unbelieving, and the abominable, and murderers, and whoremongers, and sorcerers, and idolaters, and all liars, shall have their part in the lake which burneth with fire and brimstone; which is the second death."—(Rev. xxi. 8.)

"Without (the heavenly city) are dogs, and sorcerers, and whoremongers, and murderers, and idolaters, and whosoever loveth and maketh a lie."—(Rev. xxii. 15.)

What is this but another way of saying, "Whosoever is a murderer, whosoever is a hypocrite, shall perish everlastingly"? And it is remarkable, too, that "unbelievers" are placed in the same category as murderers. But of that more anon. Is not the Dean of Westminster obliged to make the same qualifications and reservations, in passages like these, which he peremptorily repudiates in the case of the Athanasian Creed? Are all murderers, and idolaters, and liars, doomed to everlasting perdition? Do not these passages mean all murderers, idolaters, and liars *as such*—that is, all those who sin with their eyes open, and persist in their sin? If these explanations are admissible and natural in the case of Holy Scripture, why should they be dismissed as "evasions" when applied to the Athanasian Creed? But I shall have more to say on this point presently.

very neatly expressed by Pope in the well-known lines :—

> " For modes of faith let graceless zealots fight,
> His can't be wrong whose life is in the right;
> For forms of government let fools **contest,**
> Whate'er is best administered is **best.**"

It is hard to say which of these two couplets deserves the palm for shallowness of conception and viciousness of reasoning. The government which " is best administered " is not by any means necessarily " the best," as I am sure you would be the first to tell me. The best government is that which trains its subjects to govern themselves, and which thus combines the *maximum* of individual liberty with the *minimum* of governmental control. The end of all civil government is the good of the governed, and the government which approaches nearest to that end, one in which individual life is developed to the greatest extent consistent with social life, is certainly the best government. But the mere machinery of government may be, and often is, far better administered under the most grinding despotism than under the most constitutional *régime*. A people which governs itself is sure to be slower in its movements and to make more blunders than one in which the power is centred in a single person; but, on the other hand, it enjoys the inestimable blessing of freedom, it is secure against the caprice, the incapacity, or the ambition of its ruler; and its policy, on the average, is sure to be wiser, and its administration, in the long run, likely to be better.

But erroneous as Pope's view of civil government was, his maxim about "modes of faith" is still more misleading. It is, in fact, an outrageous *petitio principii*; for it begs the very point in dispute by quietly assuming that a man's life *can* be "in the right" while his creed is wrong. Now if the history of mankind tells us anything at all for certain, it is the very converse of such a proposition. Whence came we? Whither are we going? What means that mysterious inward monitor which speaks to us of right and wrong, and sounds the alarm of a future retribution? These are questions which the heart of man has been asking itself in all ages and countries, and which it cannot cease to ask till it shall cease to beat; and according to the character of the answer in each case will be the moral character of the questioner. To worship, in some shape or other, a Being supreme over human destiny is an instinct coextensive with humanity; and universal experience proves that man necessarily becomes assimilated to the object of his homage. It is so even in respect to our bodies. It is notorious that persons who live in intimate communion with each other become impressed with somewhat of one another's likeness: the stronger will impresses something of its own physical expression on the features of the weaker. The mind which *looks up* receives at length into its woof and texture, and even into its material organ, the image of the object which fascinates it. If that object be pure and ennobling it will generate a pure and noble character in the worshipper; if base and cruel, the image which it reflects must necessarily be base and cruel too. What is the history of heathendom, whether in ancient or modern times, but one long and sad illustration of this truth? And what are the gods of the pagan world, after all, and as a rule, but the sensual and cruel instincts of debased humanity deified, so that man might thus obtain a spurious sanction for the worship of self:—

"Gods partial, changeful, passionate, unjust;
Whose attributes were rage, revenge, and lust."

Such is Pope's own description of the deities of heathen mythology, and it is a proof of his shallow philosophy that he could think that a man's life could possibly be "in the right" while it succumbed to the demoralizing influences of such "modes of faith" as these. Not so thought Plato, heathen as he was. So much impressed was he with the intimate connection between a true faith and a right life that he proposed to exclude from the schools of his ideal Republic all descriptions of the Olympian deities; because "in every undertaking the beginning is the most important, especially in all that relates to the young and tender, since that is the time for receiving impressions most easily and lastingly. . . . For a child cannot distinguish between what is allegorical and what is not; and the impressions of childhood have a tendency to become fixed and indelible. Therefore we ought to consider it a matter of the utmost moment that the religious notions which children first learn should be adapted as much as possible to the promotion of virtue."*

To what a frightful pass its "modes of faith" brought the heathen world S. Paul has told us in the beginning of his Epistle to the Romans. But how was man to be restored? Where was the spell that could reclaim him from the pernicious seductions of the senses, and give him a new life? The cultivation of his intellectual faculties could not do it, for that had been tried and found wanting. Everybody would admit, I suppose, that the world has never seen a people so highly cultivated intellectually as the Athenians in the age of Pericles. But what were they morally? So foul that, as the Apostle says, "It is a shame even to speak," not merely "of those things which were done of them in secret," but of many things which were done openly in the face of day. Purity was to them simply an unknown virtue; and no wonder, for among all the gods of Olympus there was not a single deity that was pure. It is not merely that courtesans ruled society, presided at the tables of grave statesmen, and inspired the genius of an Apelles and a Praxiteles; but that impurity was actually raised to the dignity of

* Rep., b. ii., 378.

a virtue and invested with the sanctions of religion; thus indicating that abyss of depravity when the first principles of morals are not merely overthrown, but reversed,—when evil is called good and good evil. The Aphrodite Anadyomene of Apelles and the Cnidian goddess of Praxiteles were both statues of the infamous Phryne; and an image of the same courtesan was placed in the national sanctuary at Delphi without eliciting any sense of shame or profanation. The moral plague was, in fact, universal. "We have Hetairai for our pleasure," says Demosthenes in a public oration, "concubines for the ordinary requirements of the body, and wives for the procreation of lawful issue and as confidential domestic guardians."* And worse remains to be said, if it were possible to say it without shame. That hideous unnatural vice, which was the curse of most of the nations of antiquity, found in Athens a hothouse where it was forced into preternatural development. The whole literature of the Periclesian era is stained with its pestilential slime. It infested the entire framework of society, and the most eminent citizens of the time—generals, statesmen, poets, artists, and philosophers—were at once its patrons and victims. Is it possible to bring a more damaging accusation against that brilliant period of triumphant profligacy

* Κατὰ Νεαίρας. The genuineness of this oration is disputed; but, whether genuine or not, it bears witness to the immorality of the age.

than to say, what is literally true, that wherever the subject of love is mentioned in its literature it is hardly ever the love of woman that is meant? *Optimi corruptio pessima est.* Grievous indeed must have been the pestilence when such choice spirits as Plato and Socrates could not escape its contagion. The sublime unselfishness of the latter, his lofty self-restraint, his unswerving love of truth, and his noble death, will always command the admiration and reverence of good men. Yet even of him it must be sorrowfully owned that "independence of mind, not strict purity, was the leading thought of his moral teaching."* His precautions to his pupils in favour of a modified continence are never based on the sanctity of chastity or on the moral evil of impurity, but entirely on physical considerations and motives of expediency. He paid visits to the courtesan Theodota, in company with his youthful disciples, and in the most businesslike manner gave her advice as to the best mode of winning and retaining her lovers. And it shows the utter degradation of the Greek mind in this matter that Xenophon relates this licentious conversation in a work† written for the express purpose of vindicating the character of Socrates from the charge of corrupting youth. What is the inference but that chastity was not recognized as a virtue among the Athenians?

* Zeller's 'Socrates and the Socratic Schools,' translated by Reichel, p. 132.
† Mem. Soc., iii., 13.

Moreover, both in the dialogues of Plato and of Xenophon we find Socrates dallying with that abominable sin to which I have already referred, and which fortunately has no name in our language. It is clear that neither he nor Plato* regarded it as a sin at all, but rather as a lawful indulgence which was to be enjoyed in moderation. What are we to think, too, of some of the suggestions in Plato's Republic,—promiscuous concubinage, for example? Grant that even this horrible proposal was itself the bastard offspring of a sublime idea, which has found its true home and partial realization in the Church of Christ—namely, that a man should sacrifice wife, and children, and home, and friends and possessions, for the kingdom of God, which in Plato's eyes meant the State. Still the very fact that he proposed to plant the great law of self-sacrifice in the soil of social impurity is a striking proof that the idea of purity, as a virtue, had ceased to exist in the Greek mind. How much nobler and worthier is the idea of human life which Homer has portrayed in his comparatively ruder age.

We see in the example of Athens, then, a clear proof

* In justice to Plato it must be added that he does condemn it, in severe terms, in the Laws, when the experience of age had convinced him of the ravages it was committing among his countrymen. Yet even here it is probable that what Plato deplored was not so much the *moral* corruption as the deterioration of that physical beauty which the Greek loved with such passionate enthusiasm. Juvenal (Sat. ii., 10) seems to charge this vice, if not on Socrates personally, at least on his teaching.

that the cultivation of the intellect will never of itself regenerate humanity. Man is moved to action by his imagination and feelings—never by his intellect. His affections are not wrong in themselves, but in the direction in which they move and in the objects to which they cling. What they need, therefore, is a right object to attract them. Without that the sharpening of the intellect does nothing more than increase the power of the passions to indulge in wrong pursuits. "Intellect is not a power, but an instrument; not a thing which itself moves and works, but a thing which is moved and worked by forces from behind it. To say that men are ruled by reason is as irrational as to say that men are ruled by their eyes. Reason *is* an eye—the eye through which the desires see their way to gratification. And educating it only makes it a better eye—gives it a vision more accurate and more comprehensive—does not at all alter the desires subserved by it. However far-seeing you make it, the passions will still determine the directions in which it shall be turned—the objects on which it shall dwell. Just those ends which the instincts or sentiments propose will the intellect be employed to accomplish: culture of it having done nothing but increase the ability to accomplish them."*

This is an important admission, coming, as it does, from a writer who is not only one of the most profound

---

* Mr. Herbert Spencer's 'Social Statics,' p. 382.

thinkers of the day, but who, alas! does not accept the Christian Faith, though he is too much of a philosopher to erect his own unbelief into a dogma, after the common fashion of the day.

But if mere intellectual cultivation could not recall men to the "ways of pleasantness" and the paths of peace, what else could? Speaking in the rough, it may be said that three things were necessary: a right object of love; a revelation of God's will and of the true relations between man and his Maker, with a teacher having authority to enforce it; and spiritual power to enable man to "work out his own salvation." These three *desiderata* Christianity professes to have supplied.

1. Man needs a true object of affection; but such an object could be found nowhere in the ancient world outside the mountains of Judæa. Not in all the hierarchy of Olympus, nor, indeed, in any of the heathen mythologies, was there a single deity who could for a moment be the object of a pure disinterested love. It is probably for this reason that we read of no religious wars among the heathen, nor of any serious attempt at proselytism. There was not one of the falsely styled Immortals for whom any of his vassals could care to endure a moment's suffering, much less to die.

How different is the God of Israel! awful in majesty and power, and "of purer eyes than to behold iniquity;" yet yearning for the love of His creatures.

The whole range of heathen literature furnishes nothing comparable to the sweetness and beauty of the images under which Jehovah's love for His people is depicted. What can surpass the following passage in the exquisite tenderness of its pathos?

"The Lord's portion is His people; Jacob is the lot of His inheritance. He found him in a desert land, and in the waste howling wilderness. He led him about, He instructed him, He kept him as the apple of His eye. As an eagle stirreth up her nest, fluttereth over her young, spreadeth abroad her wings, taketh them, beareth them on her wings,—so the Lord alone did lead him."

Or this?—

"Behold the Lord God will come with strong hand, and His arm shall rule for Him. Behold His reward is with Him, and His work before Him. He shall feed His flock like a shepherd; He shall gather the lambs with His arm, and carry them in His bosom, and shall gently lead those that are with young."

And the ancient people of Israel, with all their backslidings, reflected back something of this Divine Love. They delighted to picture their everlasting Saviour as a Shepherd leading them through green meadows, and refreshing them "beside the waters of comfort," or as a bountiful King, "preparing a table before them in the wilderness," or "as the shadow of a great rock in a weary land." It was a love pure, unmercenary, and elevating. Their God was neither a cold abstraction, dwelling apart from His creatures in Epicurean unconcern, nor a capricious divinity who must be kept in good humour by an elaborate system of human bribes; but a Being Who watched over the fatherless and defended the cause of the widow; Who loved justice and mercy, and would "by no means clear the guilty;" Whose "mercy was over all His works," forbidding to "muzzle the ox which treadeth out the corn," to "seethe the kid in its mother's milk," or to carry off the dam bird sitting on her young. It was this combination of almighty power with lovingkindness that melted the heart of the ancient Hebrew, and weaned him at length from the corrupting influences of the nations around him. His God was not far away, but very near him; "about his path and about his bed, and spying out all his ways." He "put" the penitent's "tears into His bottle," and "in His book were all his members written." From His presence there was no escape: "If I climb up into heaven, Thou art there; if I go down to hell, Thou art there also. If I take the wings of the morning, and remain in the uttermost parts of the sea, even there shall Thy hand lead me, and Thy right hand shall hold me." And this all-embracing Presence, while it precluded all possibility of escape to the sinner, was a Presence of love and protection to the righteous. "It was a manifold, everlasting manifestation of one deep feeling—a desire for human affection. . . . . Love is not asked in vain from generous dispositions. A Being never absent, but standing beside the life of each man with ever-watchful tenderness, and recognized, though invisible, in every blessing that befel them from youth to age, became naturally the Object of their warmest affections. Their belief in Him could not exist without producing, as a necessary effect, that profound impression of passionate individual attachment which in the Hebrew authors always mingles with and vivifies their faith in the Invisible. All the books of the Old Testament are breathed upon by this breath of life."* What was it that saved Joseph in the crisis of his temptation but this feeling of "passionate individual attachment" to the God of his fathers? "How can I do this great wickedness and sin"—not against Potiphar, but—"against God?" What but the same feeling wrung that Psalm of penitential agony from the heart of David after his great sin? Uriah, Bathsheba, the scorn of his enemies, the foredoomed loss of his child, the predicted retribution on his house,—all these were swallowed up and forgotten in the one absorbing thought that he, the shepherd boy of Bethlehem, had repaid with foul ingratitude that gracious God Who had been so kind to him, Who had saved him from the lion and the bear, and given him the victory over Goliath, and delivered him from the persecution of Saul, and set him at last on the throne of Israel. "Against Thee—Thee only—

* Arthur Hallam's 'Remains,' pp. 277-8.

have I sinned, and done this evil in Thy sight." That was the thought which smote him to the earth, and which has made the 51st Psalm the model of Christian penitence throughout all time.

But, after all, it was not till the eternal Son of God appeared in the form of man that men could truly be said to have an adequate object of affection; and that for two reasons. In the first place, the idea of a Being who is infinite, yet personal; who "inhabiteth eternity," yet "dwelleth with him also that is of a contrite and humble spirit,"—is so complex that, without the concrete evidence of it which the Incarnation supplies, the multitude could never apprehend it; they would be in perpetual danger of running into the extreme of Pantheism on the one side, or of a degrading idolatry on the other. In the second place, it was only by becoming incarnate that God could fully manifest His love to the human race. In one of those wondrous adumbrations of Christianity which made some of the Fathers regard him as partially inspired, and which induced Coleridge to compare him to "a plank from the wreck of Paradise cast on the shores of idolatrous Greece," Plato declared that if Divine Wisdom would only assume a human form all mankind would fall in love with her. Like attracts like, and, to love truly, a man must feel that there is something akin to his own nature in the object of his love. For love implies sympathy, and sympathy implies a fellow-feeling, some bond of union, between the lover and the beloved. A select few among the Jews, persons of devout minds and rare spiritual insight, were able, as I have already pointed out, to realize this feeling in an intense degree even before the Incarnation. But with the mass Jehovah was an object of awe and fear and wonder rather than of loving devotion. And this was natural, for man's filial relationship to God cannot be fully realized without a belief in the Trinity. This important truth is stated with much force and clearness by Mr. Hutton, in his striking Essay on the Incarnation. " If Christ," he says, " is the Eternal Son of God, God is indeed and in essence Father; the social nature, the spring of love, is of the very essence of the Eternal Being; the communication of His life, the reciprocation of His affection, dates from beyond time —belongs, in other words, to the very being of God. Now some persons think that such a certainty even when attained has very little to do with human life. ' What does it matter,' they say, ' what the absolute nature of God is, if we know what He is *to us;* how can it concern us to know what He was before our race existed, if we know what He is to all His creatures now?' These questions seem plausible, but I believe they point to a very deep error. I can answer for myself that the Unitarian conviction that God is—*as* God and in His Eternal Essence—a single and, so to say, solitary personality, influenced my imagination and the whole colour of my faith most profoundly. Such a conviction, thoroughly reached, renders it impossible to identify any of the social attributes with His real *essence*— renders it difficult not to regard power as the true root of all other divine life. If we are to believe that the Father was from all time, we must believe that He was *as* a Father—that is, that love was actual in Him as well as potential, that the communication of life and thought and fulness of joy was of the inmost nature of God, and never began to be if God never began to be.

"For my own part, I am sure that our belief, whatever it may be, about the 'absolute' nature of God, influences far more than any one supposes our practical thoughts about the actual relation of God to us. Unitarians eagerly deny—I once eagerly denied—that God is to them a solitary omnipotence. Nor is he. But I am sure that the conception of a single eternal will as originating, and infinitely antecedent to, all acts of love or spiritual communion with any other, affects vitally the temper of their faith. The throne of heaven is to them a lonely one. The solitude of the eternities weighs upon their imaginations. *Social* are necessarily postponed to *individual* attributes; for they date from a later origin—from creation,—while power and thought are eternal. Necessarily, therefore, God, though spoken of and worshipped as a Father to us, is conceived *primarily* as imagining and creating; secondarily only, as loving and inspiring. But any Being,

Whose thoughts and resolves are conceived as in any sense deeper than His affections, is necessarily regarded rather as benignant and compassionate than as affording the type of that deepest kind of love which is coordinate with life;—in short, rather as a beneficence whose love springs out of power and reason, than as one Whose power and reason are grounded in love. I am sure that this notion of God as the Absolute Cause does tincture deeply even the highest form of Unitarian faith, and I cannot see how it could be otherwise. If our prayers are addressed to One Whose eternity we habitually image as unshared, we necessarily for the time merge the Father in the Omniscient and Omnipotent genius of the universe. If, on the other hand, we pray to One Who has revealed His own eternity through the Eternal Son—if in the spirit of the Liturgies, Catholic and Protestant, we alternate our prayers to the eternal originating Love, and to that Filial Love in which it has been eternally mirrored, turning from the 'Father of heaven' to the 'Son, Redeemer of the world,' and back again to Him in Whom that Son for ever rests—then we keep a God essentially *social* before our hearts and minds, and fill our imagination with no solitary grandeur."[*]

But true as all this is, it may be doubted whether the doctrine of the Trinity, if revealed without the In-

---

[*] 'Essays, Theological and Literary.' By R. H. Hutton, i., pp. 246-8.

carnation of the Second Person, would ever have had any appreciable influence on the conduct of mankind at large. "God is Love," and the essence of love is self-sacrifice. But how was this idea, which lies at the root of the Christian conception of God, to be made operative in the sphere of human conduct? Only by the fulfilment of Plato's dream. Divine Love must take a human form in order to attract the love of men. Is it too bold a paradox to say that, incapable as God is of suffering, yet if He would reveal His nature to us He must show Himself as a Sufferer? And since it was impossible that He could do this in His Divine Essence, it was necessary that He should take into everlasting union with His own a nature which was capable of suffering. God is ever sacrificing Himself; being essentially Love, He cannot do otherwise. But His self-sacrifice involves no pain, because His life is a perfect life. Our self-sacrifice is painful because it involves conflict with our inherent selfishness. In God there is no selfishness, and therefore His perpetual self-sacrifice is perpetual joy. We dread pain and flee from suffering. Nevertheless "pain," as Arthur Hallam* truly observes, "is the deepest thing we have in our nature," for it is a continual reminder that our life is diseased, and that if we would "save" it "unto life eternal" we must consent to "lose" it under its temporal conditions. And hence the Epiphany of the Eternal God in the

* 'Remains,' p. 281.

manger of Bethlehem. It was a manifestation of absolute unselfishness. He "emptied Himself" of His incommunicable perfections, "by taking the form of a slave and appearing in the likeness of men." The Lord of all became the slave of all; "the Prince of Life" became the victim of death; He, Whose are "all the beasts of the forest and the cattle on a thousand hills," became a houseless wanderer in Judea; He "with Whom is the well of life" sued the adulterous woman of Samaria for a drink at Jacob's well; He Who is the Judge of quick and dead was condemned to a cruel and degrading death before a human tribunal. Nor was it on occasion merely that He gave proof of His self-sacrifice. What was His whole life on earth but one act of self-sacrifice? He lavished the bounties of His exhaustless treasures freely upon others; He never once used His power to save Himself trouble or pain:—

> "Poor He became, and left His glorious seat
> To make us humble and to make us great;
> His business here was happiness to give
> To those whose malice would not let Him live.
>
> *   *   *   *   *
>
> Who for Himself no miracle would make
> Dispensed with several for the peoples' **sake.**
> He that, long-fasting, would no wonder show,
> Made loaves and fishes, as they eat them, grow.
>
> Of all His power, which boundless was above,
> Here He used none but to express His love;

And such a love would make our joy exceed,
Not when our own, but others', mouths we feed.

* * * * *

Love as He loved! A love so unconfined
With arms extended would embrace mankind.
Self-love would cease, or be dilated, when
We should behold as many selfs as men."

      WALLER's *Poem of Divine Love.*

2. And this law of total self-surrender He taught "with authority and not as the Scribes." "His word was with power." He found the rule of selfishness in possession of the world; might everywhere triumphant over right. It is difficult to realize in a Christian land how utterly the duty of self-sacrifice was ignored in the social and political life of the ancient world. The domination of the selfish principle in public and private life is embedded in the very language of the most law-abiding and the most moral of the nations of the Old World. In Latin, as every schoolboy knows, the word for enemy means literally a stranger, and *rivals* meant originally persons inhabiting the opposite banks of a stream; as if every stranger must needs be an enemy, and every stream a sufficient excuse for strife to those whom it divided! And such, in sober fact, was the condition of the world when our Lord appeared. Self reigned supreme in the relations of nation with nation, and of man with man; and wherever its outward manifestation was repressed it was not from the love of man for God or his neighbour, but from motives of fear and

self-interest. The **spirit remained** unchanged, and so man remained the **same.**

This evil spirit **Christ** smote **with the** opposite spirit of entire unselfishness. He "came not **to do His own will," He** said, but **to** "lay down His life a ransom for many." While "the foxes had holes and the birds **of the** air had nests," He, their Lord and Master, "had not where to lay His head." And the self-denial which He practised Himself He imposed upon His followers. They were to welcome suffering, **not** merely to endure it when it came. They were *to take up* their crosses, **not** simply bear them when laid on their unwilling backs. They were to *love* their enemies and do them good instead of resting satisfied with a merely passive forgiveness. They were even to "rejoice and be exceeding" glad when men persecuted and reviled them. Moreover, they were not to "lay up treasures upon earth," but rather to "seek first the kingdom of God and His righteousness," in the confidence that, if they did so, all that was good for them in their earthly life would be supplied to them by their heavenly Father.

That this was a new doctrine is evident from the reception **which** the world gave it. It was described **as a** doctrine that was "turning the world upside down." And the description was scarcely **an** exaggeration. Christianity really did turn the world "upside down." It reversed the direction of human feeling and the rule of human conduct. **It** was with a true instinct, therefore, that the Roman Empire fought such a desperate battle against it; for Christianity and Roman Imperialism were essentially incompatible. The triumph of the one meant the destruction of the other. And, so far, Christianity was a revolutionary religion. It was a reformation on the largest scale possible, and every reformation which claims to be radical (in the etymological sense of the word) must wear more or less of a revolutionary aspect to its own generation. This is unavoidable; for the only way to achieve a great and lasting reform, be it social, political, or religious, is to convert the multitude; and that can only be done by enlisting their imagination on the side of a few great principles which they can easily comprehend and digest, leaving time and circumstances to supply the necessary qualifications. Hence it is that all reformers worthy of the name are, as a rule, regarded as revolutionists by the conservative portion of their contemporaries. They find it impossible to overcome the obstacles which beset their path without an impulse from the popular sentiment, and so they project into the arena of public discussion a few broad principles, easily understood and easily remembered, but requiring a certain moderation and discretion in the application of them. If a reformer were to qualify his propositions with every imaginable exception, and make them so smooth and round that they would pass through the mind without scratching it, the result would be that they would make no impression at all, and no reformation could ever take place.

But revolutionary as Christianity was deemed by those who witnessed its nascent struggles for victory, it was, in truth, the most conservative of all religions, —conservative, that is, of all that is worth preserving in the social, political, and individual life of man. It differed from all other religions, before or since, in this, that it planted fruitful and enduring principles in the heart of humanity instead of prescribing a code of rules; and those principles, in proportion as they have had a fair field, have erected on the ruins of ancient polities a fairer civilization than Pagan poet or philosopher ever dreamt of. Christianity, and it alone, has thus realized the poet's words: its influence on the world has been that of a " pure religion breathing household laws:" not teaching, or professing to teach, a new art of living, but *breathing* a spirit into human nature which should have a continual and an increasing tendency to exorcise its innate selfishness and make it pregnant with the seeds of righteous laws. It made no overt war on any of the institutions of the time, or of any time; but it disseminated principles which struck their roots beneath the decaying systems of Paganism, so that, when they fell, the " Civitas Dei " was ready to take their place. Neither slavery nor despotism is proscribed in set terms in the New Testament. But both are implicitly condemned by the proclamation of the equality of all men in Christ and of the responsibility of rulers to the Supreme Judge of all; and the result has been that slavery, whether social or political, has succumbed, surely if slowly, to the influence of Christian ideas. " Slavery, in the age of the Apostles, had so penetrated society, was so intimately woven with it, and the materials of servile war were so abundant, that a religion preaching freedom to the slave would have shaken the social fabric to its foundations, and would have armed against itself the whole power of the State. Paul did not then assail the institution. He satisfied himself with spreading principles which, however slowly, could not but work its destruction."*

And what is true of slavery is equally true of a great many other things. " In Christianity," says one of the deepest thinkers and ablest writers of our generation, " the rules are so comprehensive and large as uniformly to furnish the major premiss of a syllogism; whilst the particular act under discussion, wearing perhaps some modern name, naturally is not directly mentioned: and to bring this, in the minor proposition, under the principle contained in the major is a task left to the judgment of the inquirer in each particular case. Some-

* Channing, quoted by Mr. Goldwin Smith in 'Does the Bible Sanction American Slavery?' p. 103.

thing is here entrusted to individual understanding; whereas in the Koran, from the circumstantiality of the rule, you are obliged mechanically to rest in the letter of the precept. The Christian Scriptures therefore not only teach, but train the mind to habits of *self*-teaching in all moral questions, by enforcing more or less of activity in applying the rule; that is, in subsuming the given case proposed under the Scriptural principle."*

It is not merely the abolition of slavery, then, that has followed in the wake of Christianity. From the very first Christianity prescribed monogamy as the rule of its converts, and from that moment marriage became a sacred thing. Woman ceased to be the slave of man's passions or the toy of his caprice; she became his partner in a mystical union which only death could sunder, and thus exercised a purifying influence in the regeneration of society which it is hardly possible to exaggerate—an influence which simply did not exist in any part or form of heathen society. War has not been abolished by Christianity; but it has ceased to characterize the chronic relations of nations to each other. Public opinion has stamped it as an execrable crime, and Christian influences have done much to mitigate its horrors. It may safely be predicted that it will be a long time before we hear again of a Christian Government en-

---

* De Quincey's Works, vol. xi., pp. 278-9. This characteristic of Christianity has also been well stated by the author of 'Ecce Homo,' chap. xiii.

gaging in war "with a light heart;" and we may reasonably hope that the example which England and America have just set of referring international disputes to the arbitration of reason and justice, rather than to the barbarous arbitrament of the sword, will not be lost on the world. The Treaty of Washington marks an era in civilization. Its influence will not be destroyed by any temporary misadventure, and we may trust that the policy which it represents will, at no distant day, take its place in the code of international morality.

The intrinsic sacredness of human life is another legacy from the Incarnation of the Son of God. Infanticide was not considered a crime against eternal morality by the most advanced races of the heathen world, and among the less advanced it was a recognized law of political economy—the most sensible and rational expedient for getting rid of superfluous or useless population. Even Plato did not scruple to prescribe abortion and infanticide, in certain cases, among the laws of his "Republic." Misshapen and sickly children, and the children of aged and diseased parents—all children, in fact, which were likely not to make good citizens, were to be ruthlessly exposed on the mountains, to perish either of cold and hunger or by the fangs of hungry wolves.

But the Incarnate Son sanctified every condition of life through which He passed, and since He became a wailing infant the helplessness of childhood has always been considered an additional claim on the protection of

I

manhood. We are still far from an adequate recognition of the heinousness of recklessly destroying the lives of beings made in the image of God and redeemed by His blood. But we are separated by a whole continent of thought and feeling from the time when a Roman Emperor could, on a summer's afternoon, put twenty thousand slaves to death " to make a Roman holiday."

Another creation of Christianity is the sense of responsibility with which all Christian nations now govern their subject races; and in this matter our own country has taken an honourable lead. The impeachment of Warren Hastings, in the name of the Commons of England, "for high crimes and misdemeanours" against the people of India, bore no visible fruit at the time, and Burke died in the belief that his transcendent effort was, after all, a failure. But it was no failure. His fiery denunciation of wrong and of oppression sank into the public conscience and leavened the thought of Europe; and "he, being dead, yet speaketh" in the recent punishment, by a Viceroy of India, of two English subordinates, for putting to death, without legal trial, a handful of native rebels. In what state of heathen antiquity would such a thing have been possible? In Rome, whose greatest Viceroy put a million Gauls to death, and sold another million into slavery?* But who can read Burke's speeches against Warren Hastings without seeing that he drew all his inspiration

* Goldwin Smith's 'Lectures on Modern History,' lect. iii., p. 39.

from the spirit of the Gospel? This it was which caused his pity for the people of India, and roused his mind to a frenzy of indignation against their wrongs. In truth, the great principles of Christian morality are now so interwoven with our tone of mind and habits of thought, that we act on them unconsciously, often attributing to the exercise of a sound political judgment modes of action and rules of government which, but for the silent infiltration of Christian influences, we should never have thought of.

We are sometimes told, by men of superficial reading or impatient tempers, that the Christian Church has been a foe to political freedom. In fact, it has been the parent and nourisher of political freedom. De Quincey is unquestionably right when he says that "the Greeks and Romans, although so frantically republican, and, in *some* of their institutions, so democratic, yet, on the other hand, never developed the idea of representative government. The elective principle was widely known among them. . . . Public authority and jurisdiction were created and modified by the elective principle; but never was this principle applied to the creation or direction of public opinion. . . . Strange, indeed, that so mighty a secret as that of delegating public opinions to the custody of elect representatives, a secret which has changed the face of the world, should have been missed by nations applying so vast an energy to the whole theory of public administration. But the truth, however paradoxical, is that in Greece and Rome no body of public opinions existed that could have furnished a standing-ground for adverse parties. In all the dissensions of Rome, from the secession of the Plebs to the factions of the Gracchi, of Marius and Sylla, of Cæsar and Pompey; in all the στάσεις of the Grecian republics,—the contest could no more be described as a contest of opinion than could the feuds of our buccaneers in the seventeenth century, when parting company, or fighting for opposite principles of dividing the general booty."*

"Does Christianity interfere with political progress?" asks Mr. Goldwin Smith.† "The instrument of political progress is generally allowed to be liberty. It is allowed to be so ultimately even by those who wish to suppress it provisionally, and to inaugurate for the present a despotic dictatorship of their own ideas. And Christianity, by first proclaiming the equality and brotherhood of men, became the parent of just and enduring liberty. What spiritual power prevailed over the birth of our free institutions? Was it not the earnest though narrow and distorted Christianity of the Middle Ages, which still, though its hour is past, shows its ancient spirit in Montalembert? What power was it that directly consecrated the principle of local self-government, the foundation of all true liberty, in the religious association of the parish? Cast your eyes

* Works, vol. xi., p. 273. † Lect. iii., p. 32.

over the map of Europe, and see whether sincere Christianity and political freedom are unsuited to dwell together. Name, if you can, any great Christian philosopher who has been an enemy to freedom. On the other hand, Hobbes, Bolingbroke, Hume, Gibbon, were Imperialists; they all belonged, though in different degrees, to the school which takes a sensual and animal view of man, mistrusts all moral and spiritual restraints, and desires a strong despotism to preserve tranquillity, refinement, and the enjoyments and conveniences of life. It need not be added that the most fanatical enemies of Christianity at the present day are also fanatical Imperialists."

I have quoted these two distinguished and learned writers, the one a strong Tory, the other a Liberal of the most advanced type, not only because they have expressed my own thoughts in much better language than I can command, but because, being laymen, they cannot be suspected of any professional bias, and are, moreover, free from every tinge of what it is now the fashion to stigmatize as "Sacerdotalism." Both De Quincey and Mr. Goldwin Smith contend that not political progress alone, but progress of every kind, "intellectual or industrial," is indebted to Christianity. Stock arguments, like that from the persecution of Galileo, merely prove that Christianity, like Nature, has now and then been misinterpreted by fallible and impatient zealots. Theologians have not by any means been the most successful opponents of scientific discoveries. The chief obstructives have been men of science themselves. Harvey's 'Exercitatio de Motu Cordis' was greeted as an outrageous paradox by the Medical Profession; and, in fact, every great discovery in medical science has had to fight its way against the prejudices (not always confined to words) of the Faculty. And so it has fared with other sciences. It has been true of most of them that "a man's foes are they of his own household." I am not quite sure that even in these days of enlightened toleration a scientific discovery which ran violently counter to received opinion would not have to reckon with the only persecution which is now possible—railing and ridicule. But science is not responsible for the mistakes of its advocates, nor is Christianity necessarily compromised by the ignorant zeal of its champions.

I might go on to show that charitable institutions of every kind have grown up under the shadow of the Cross. The Sacrifice of Calvary has established a kind of sympathy even between man and the lower creation. Societies against cruelty to animals would have been considered a premonitory symptom of insanity till He appeared Whose providential care is over the sparrows, and Who "feedeth the young ravens that call upon Him." Nor was it till man learnt that the whole creation "groaneth and travaileth in pain together" with himself, and is a sharer alike in his Fall and his Redemption, that Nature became an object of reverent contemplation to the philosopher, the poet, and the painter. Certainly, as a matter of fact, Physical Science owes its splendid triumphs partly to that spirit of self-devotion which is the child of the Incarnation, and partly to that feeling of mysterious sympathy between man and Nature which is one of the fruits of Christianity. In the light of Revelation the material world has ceased to be regarded as "a fortuitous concourse of atoms." All its life and all its glory are seen to be from Him in Whom not mankind only, but all things, "live, and move, and have their being." He created it in the beginning, and He sustains it from moment to moment by His omnipresent will. Under the dominion of this feeling the poet and the painter now regard Nature with other eyes than those of the ancients. In the varied and entrancing beauties of earth and sea and sky, in the mystery of the forest and the ocean, in the joyousness of the dawn and the pensive beauty of evening, they find the evidence of a mysterious Presence—

> " Whose dwelling is the light of setting suns,
> And the round ocean, and the living air,
> And the blue sky, and in the mind of man :—
> A motion and a spirit, which impels
> All thinking things, all objects of all thought,
> And rolls through all things."

" When a modern, instead of writing modern poetry, imitates, however skilfully, the poetry of the Greeks, how great is the sacrifice of all that most touches our hearts; and yet how much that is beyond the range of Greek sentiment remains! Philanthropy is a Greek word, but how wide a circle of ideas does its present meaning embrace! In natural religion itself the progress seems not less clear. Man's idea of God must rise as he sees more of Him in His works, as he sees more of Him by reflecting on his own nature (in which the true proof of natural religion lies), and in those efforts of human virtue in other men which would be unaccountable if there were no God, and this world were all. More and more, too, from age to age, the ideas of the soul and of a future life rise in distinctness; Man feels more and more that he is a traveller between the cradle and the grave, and that the great fact of life is death; and the centre of human interest moves gradually towards the other world." On the other hand, "the Greek, for the most part, rose lightly from the banquet of life to pass into that unknown land with whose mystery speculation had but dallied, and of which comedy had made a jest. The Roman lay down almost as lightly to rest after his course of public duty. But now if death could really regain his victory in the mind of man, hunger and philosophy together would hardly hold life in its course. The latest and most thorough-going school of materialism has found it necessary to provide something for man's spiritual nature, and has made a shadowy divinity out of the abstract being of humanity, and a shadowy immortality of the soul out of a figment that the dead are greater than the living. Lucretius felt no such need."*

By becoming incarnate, then, God the Son **not only** provided an adequate object of human affections; He extended **immeasurably** the whole horizon of our thoughts, our hopes, our aspirations. He gave back to man the Sceptre over Nature which the Fall in Eden had wrested from his hand, and, in earnest of our final triumph over the forces which now govern our material organism and to which it must one day succumb, He made the laws of matter subservient to His Human Will. He turned water into wine, and multiplied indefinitely and in a moment the produce alike of earth and sea. He walked on liquid water as upon solid ground, and by one royal word calmed at once the fear of His disciples and the angry waves of the Lake of Galilee. At His touch diseases fled, and Death yielded up his prey at His command. And this control over **Nature** He delegated, in a measure, to redeemed Humanity. The old enmity was to cease; man was to resume his original supremacy, and Nature was to do him service. "Thou madest him to have dominion over the works of Thy hands, and Thou hast put all things in subjection under his feet." This dominion, which was forfeited by

---

* Goldwin Smith 'On the Study of History,' p. 38. Cf. Oxenham on 'The Catholic Doctrine of the Atonement,' second edition, p. 306.

the First Adam, was won back for humanity by the perfect obedience of the Second. The Second Head of our race refused "all the kingdoms of the world and the glory of them" when the Tempter offered them as a bribe for sinful service; and now they are His by the noble title of conquest by the Cross. "The kingdoms of the world have become the kingdoms of our Lord and of His Christ;" and the Carpenter of Nazareth is at this moment the acknowledged Lord and King of the ruling nations of the world. The legend on Constantine's fiery cross is being still fulfilled; for from his time to our own the great pioneers of human progress have conquered in the sign of the Cross. Even in the realm of Nature how marvellous are the triumphs which Christendom, and Christendom alone, has achieved! The language of the Psalmist is no longer an exaggeration; for may we not say of man, with some degree of truth, that God "has put all things in subjection under his feet"? In answer to his eager questioning the earth is revealing day by day the hoary record of her chequered history, and the sea has been made to disclose the secrets of its mysterious depths; the very lightning has been imprisoned, like the Geni in Eastern fable, and been compelled to become the obedient messenger of man's behests. Where, indeed, shall his triumphs end who has already measured the stars, and calculated their movements, and analyzed their properties?

To what are these wonderful achievements mainly

due? Is it by accident that they are connected with Christianity? Or must we not rather say that they ought in justice to be ascribed to that stimulus which the Christian Revelation necessarily imparted to human progress by elevating the vision of mankind, and expanding indefinitely, and in all directions, its field of view? Without that Revelation what inducement had man to investigate Nature or to break down the barriers which she interposed between the mutual intercourse of races and nations? The creature of a day, the sport of circumstances, ignorant alike of the destinies of his race and of his own origin and end, why should he trouble himself about the forces of Nature further than to provide as well as he could against their encroachments on his comfort? Seeing in every foreigner a natural enemy, why should he take pains to facilitate the intercommunion of peoples and tribes? Mr. Palgrave tells us that among the tribes of the interior of Africa there is a proverb which says that "Trade is war." But by the proclamation of the common brotherhood of all men, under one Master who died for all and lives for all, Trade is peace, and nations find that they are necessary to each other, and that "if one member suffers, all the members suffer with it."

3. But something more was yet required for the regeneration of humanity. Man needed an object of love on which his heart might repose securely; he needed a revelation of God's will and of his own place in the

universe. But he also needed health; for he was sick, and there was no balm in all the laboratory of human Science that could heal him of his wounds. Christ came, therefore, **not as "the** Desire of all nations" merely, and not merely as the Teacher of men, but, above all, as the Healer of our race. He came, not to develop our nature, but to make it new; to reconstruct it from the foundation; to place a new organic force at the centre of our being, which should gradually transform our nature into the likeness of His own. Humanity had been perverted from its true end, but it was still divine; else the Son **of God could not** have clothed Himself in it. The very misery **of man** proved, in fact, his grandeur, as Pascal observed long ago. There is an unearthly melody **in** his song, and something more than mortal mingles **in** his wail. Natures inferior to his may be miserable; but they are not conscious of their own misery. The knowledge of his misery adds poignancy to man's sorrow, but it also bears testimony to the high estate from which he is fallen. He is like a dethroned monarch, bearing about him in his exile the lineaments of his royal birth.

> " The soul that rises with us, our life's star,
>   **Hath had** elsewhere **its** setting,
>   And cometh from afar:
>   Not in entire forgetfulness,
>   And **not** in utter nakedness,
>   But trailing clouds of glory do we come
>   **From God, Who is our** home."

It was one of the fundamental errors of the leaders of the Reformation on the Continent that they utterly denied that man "trailed" any "clouds of glory" from his heavenly home. They taught that the Fall vitiated human nature at the very core, making it altogether corrupt, so that God could find nothing in it but what was abominable and hateful. That this is no exaggeration of their teaching a few quotations will show:—

"Let us," says Calvin, "grasp this unquestionable truth which no opposition can ever shake, that the mind of man is so completely alienated from the righteousness of God, that it conceives, desires, and undertakes everything that is impious, perverse, base, flagitious; that his heart is so thoroughly infected by the poison of sin that it cannot produce anything but what is corrupt; and that if, at any time, men do anything apparently good, yet the mind always remains involved in hypocrisy and deceitful obliquity, and the heart remains enslaved by its inward perverseness. . . . In vain do we look in our nature for anything that is good."*

Again:—

"Everything in man, the understanding and the will, the soul and body, is polluted. . . . Man is, of himself, nothing but concupiscence."†

* Instit., lib. ii., c. 3, § 19. The title of this chapter is *Ex corruptâ hominis naturâ nihil nisi damnabile prodire.*

† Ibid., lib. ii., c. 1, § 10.

Again :—

"Man cannot be excited or biassed to anything but what is evil. If this is so, there is no impropriety in affirming that he is under the necessity of sinning."*

This goes the whole length of making God the author of evil. And Calvin does not shrink from that terrible alternative. He scouts as a miserable evasion the idea that sin takes place by the permission of God, and not by His active volition. He affirms that neither wicked men, nor even the devil, "can do anything but by the secret will of God." And he quotes, as illustrations in point, the "lying spirit" in the mouth of Ahab's prophets and the incest of Absalom.† "Man," he says, "by a just impulse of God, does what is wrong."‡

Melancthon and Zuingli use the same language as Calvin. The former maintains that the virtues of good heathens, the constancy of Socrates, the chastity of Xenocrates, the temperance of Zeno, were not virtues at all, but "must be considered as vices;"§ and that, in fact, "all the works of men and all their endeavours are sinful." He too, like Calvin, accepts the full consequences of his premisses, and does not scruple to make God the direct author of sin, citing, by way of illustration, the adultery of David, which he maintains was

---

* Instit., lib. ii., c. 3, § 5.   † Ibid., lib. i., c. 18, § 4.
‡ Ibid., lib. iv., c. 18, § 2.
§ "Non debent pro veris virtutibus sed pro vitiis haberi." *Loci Theologici*, p. 22.

inspired by God, yet without sin.* Zuingli uses the same illustration, and for the same purpose. God, he says, is "the author, mover, and impeller" of the sins and crimes which men commit.† Beza maintained that God actually creates a portion of mankind for the express purpose of making them his instruments in working evil. He does not **merely** suffer them to do **wrong**, nor merely **rules the event**; He literally incites, impels, **moves and governs them in the execution of** their wicked designs.‡ It followed, of course, that **man had** really no free will properly so called, and both Calvinists and Lutherans accepted, without hesitation, that corollary from their doctrine. Yet, with singular want of logic for so logical a mind, Calvin asserted that God was angry with His creatures and intended mischief against them for sins which they were predestined **and** created to commit, and which therefore **they could not**

---

* The passage is so coarse that I must leave it in its Latin disguise: "Quod Deus facit libere facit, alienus ab omni affectu noxio, igitur et absque peccato, ut adulterium David, *quod ad auctorem Deum pertinet, non magis Deo sit peccatum quam cum taurus totum armentum inscendit et implet.*"

† "Unum igitur atque idem **facinus**, puta adulterium aut homicidium, quantum **Dei auctoris, motoris,** impulsoris, opus est, crimen non est, quantum autem hominis **est** crimen ac scelus est." *De Provid.*, c. vi. I cannot conceive any doctrine more utterly subversive of morality than this.

‡ "Sic autem agit (Deus) **per illa instrumenta, ut** non tantum sinat **illa agere, nec** tantum moderetur eventum, **sed etiam** incitet, impellat, moveat, regat, atque adeo, quod omnium est maximum, et **creat ut per illa agat quod constituit.**" *Aphorism*, xxii.

possibly have helped. "No man can contemplate himself," he says, "and seriously consider his own character without perceiving that God is angry and at enmity with him; and consequently he must see that he is bound anxiously to find some method of appeasing Him."*

The Lutherans took much the same view of the Fall as the Calvinists, though they rejected the Calvinistic theory of Predestination. They held that the Fall actually deprived man of an essential part of humanity, and injected a certain evil substance into his nature. The image of God was not merely marred, but absolutely extinguished, and the image of the Devil—a positive element of evil—was substituted in its room.†
In propagating such a view Luther is certainly open to Moehler's censure, that he "here touched on the borders of Manicheism, if he did not actually overstep the frontier." Having thus reduced man to what

---

* Instit., b. iii., c. 22, § 7.

† Moehler's 'Symbolism,' translated by Robertson, pp. 77–88. Moehler quotes the following opinions of Luther on this subject:—
"It is the nature of man to sin; sin constitutes the essence of man; the nature of man, since his fall, is become quite changed; original sin is that very thing which is born of father and mother." "The clay out of which we are born is damnable; the fœtus in its mother's womb is sin." "Man, as he is born of his father and mother, together with his whole nature and essence, is not only a sinner, but sin itself." These extravagant and horrible opinions find no place in the theology of the leading Lutherans of our day. See Müller 'On the Christian Doctrine of Sin,' *passim.*

Hallam calls "a degraded Caliban,"* Luther invented the figment of an imputed righteousness—a cloak, not a cure, for the sores of humanity. "God," he says, "sent His Son into the world, and laid upon Him all the sins of all men, saying, 'Be thou Peter, that denier; Paul, that persecutor, blasphemer, and cruel oppressor; David that adulterer; be thou that sinner that ate the apple in Paradise; that thief which hung upon the Cross: in short, be thou the person who has committed the sins of all men. See, therefore, that thou pay and satisfy them.' . . . Therefore where sins are seen and felt they are no longer sins." † To say that faith without works was dead and unprofitable he pronounced "a devilish and blasphemous doctrine," and accordingly his reverence for the Bible did not prevent him from denouncing the Epistle of S. James as "an Epistle of straw."

It is the natural tendency of all reformers to bend, by the force of the recoil, towards the opposite extreme to that from which they are escaping. While, therefore, we repudiate the doctrines of the Continental Reformers we may make allowance for them personally, and charitably put down to the circumstances in which they found themselves, rather than to any moral obliquity in themselves, opinions which strike at the root, not of Christianity alone, but of Theism altogether. At

* 'Hist. of Lit.,' iii., p. 284.
† Comment. on Gal., chap. iii., verse 13.

K

the same time we cannot be too grateful that their peculiar views on the Fall and Redemption of Man have, after all, left so little taint on our own Anglican theology. They have, indeed, to a considerable degree, stained the imagination of a large portion of the community, and I am persuaded that if we could trace the popular objections to the Athanasian Creed back to their source, we should find that they arise not so much from anything in the Creed itself as from foreign ideas imported into it from Calvinistic and Lutheran theology.

Discarding that theology, therefore, let us consider very briefly what is really meant by the doctrine of the Fall. "For," as Coleridge truly observes, "without just and distinct views respecting the Article of Original Sin it is impossible to understand aright any of the peculiar doctrines of Christianity."*

I have already referred to that law of human character which made it necessary that man should be created with a will in a state of imperfect development, but capable of self-determined fixity in one of two moral conditions. We are not to suppose, however, that Adam's will before the Fall was in a state of simple neutrality. It is the teaching of the Church that, in addition to that aggregate of natural endowments which we possess in common with him, and which constitute the integrity of human nature, our

* 'Aids to Reflection,' p. 215.

First Parents possessed a gift of Supernatural Grace, sufficiently powerful to sway the will in the right direction, but not strong enough to interfere with its essential freedom. On man's disobedience this supernatural endowment was withdrawn; not necessarily by way of punishment, but rather, perhaps, because it would be hurtful to him in his fallen condition. For, according to the common proverb, "What is one man's meat is another man's poison;" the food that nourishes and invigorates the healthy may prove fatal to one that is sickly. Adam, by his transgression, severed his will from that of his Maker, and started aside into the isolation of self-assertion; consequently he became incapable of direct communion with God, and was therefore banished from the Divine Presence, lest the "flaming sword" should destroy him. "For our God is a consuming fire;" and necessarily so to all who are ungodly. We may see a parable of this impressive truth in the incident of the Burning Bush on Horeb. The Bush "burned with fire, and the Bush was not consumed." But the moment Moses "turned aside" and approached the flame of the Divine Presence, he was warned off instantly, urgently. "Moses! Moses! Draw not nigh hither." Why was this? Because God is necessarily "a consuming fire,"—as Moses afterwards calls Him, probably with reference to this very incident,—to everything which is antagonistic to His nature. There is nothing antagonistic to Him in the productions and operations of Nature—" He hath given them a law which shall not be **broken**," and therefore they can bear **contact** with His Presence and **not** be consumed. But **in** the best of men there is an element of selfishness,—that **is, of** opposition to the Divine Nature, which is absolutely unselfish. Therefore God deals mercifully with **us,** as he dealt with Moses of old when he desired to see His glory. "Thou canst not see **My face**; for there shall no man see Me and live. And the Lord said, Behold, there is a place **by Me,** and thou shalt stand upon a rock; and it shall **come to** pass, while My glory passeth by, that I will **put thee** in a clift of the rock, and will cover thee with **My** hand while I pass by; and I will take away My hand, and **thou** shalt see My back parts: but My face shall not be seen." Such is the condition of humanity now. It is "in a clift of the rock," covered with God's hand, and beholding "the back parts" of His passing glory, but not daring as yet to look on His surpassing beauty, lest the vision, like Semele's, should consume it. For, **as there** may be what Milton calls "darkness from **excessive** bright," **so** it is possible that in our present condition the Beatific **Vision,** which makes the happiness of saints and angels, **might** fill us with intolerable pain. Even the contemplation of earthly beauty is sometimes felt **to be** painful. Sir John Herschel tells us that when he saw Sirius coming on in all its glory he was obliged **to turn away from** his telescope and shut his eyes on the beautiful sight. And so the promise to "see the King in His beauty" is only to those who are "pure in heart," and who shall be privileged hereafter to "look upon the land that is very far off." Here we must be content to "see through a glass darkly," and adore behind a veil of sacramental agency.

On Adam's fall, then, the "Donum Supernaturale" was withdrawn, for by his transgression man had closed up the avenues through which it acted. He had altered, so to speak, the centre of gravity in his constitution, and disorganized his whole system. The unity of his complex nature was broken, for its ruling principle, the will, had broken loose from the attraction of the Sun of Righteousness, and become the slave of every passing influence. Humanity still remained in its integrity, nor was any substantive element of evil introduced into it. And yet a great change had passed over it. It "became subject to vanity." Its affections were perverted from their proper objects, the spiritual faculties were therefore starved of their proper nutriment, and their development was consequently arrested. They were feeble, emaciated and dwarfed, and had not strength sufficient to resist the earthward attraction of the senses.

Christ came to reverse this downward attraction. He came to be "the Way, the Truth, and the Life," that is, to place humanity in connection with a new object of attraction, and in communication with a new source and principle of life. The old channels had been dammed up by man's sin; the old trunk had become well nigh sapless, and was hastening to decay. Therefore a New Head of our race appeared as the True Vine on which the members of the Old Man might be engrafted, and from which they might derive spiritual nourishment. "As in Adam all die, even so in Christ shall all be made alive." How did all men die in Adam? Was it not by deriving from him a perverted life? How are they to be made alive in Christ? Is it not by receiving from Him the germ of a perfect life, which, if they do not resist its influence, will so leaven their old nature that it will become gradually transformed into the image of the Second Adam? The remedy must cover the disease; the Redemption in Christ must be commensurate with the Fall in Adam; else the Gospel is a fiction and Christianity a dream. From the First Adam we inherited a depraved life: the fact must be admitted even by those who refuse to admit its cause. It is with no heritage of *imputed* ills that we are born, but with a very real perversion of our natural faculties; and it is by no figment of an *imputed* righteousness that we are to be saved, but by a veritable participation in the Redeemed Humanity of our Incarnate Lord. We are to be made, and not merely accounted, righteous. Unless we admit that we are really and actually partakers of Christ's Humanity, partakers in a sense as real as our participation in the corrupt humanity of Adam, a great deal of the language of the New Testament becomes irrelevant and misleading rhetoric. What is the meaning of the antithesis, which runs through S. Paul's Epistles, between the First Adam and the Second, the Old Man and the New, unless we are to understand that each is a fountain-head of humanity—the one, of the humanity which fell in Eden, the other, of the humanity which triumphed on the Cross?

Now our connection with fallen humanity is an organic connection; the First Adam has passed on his own injured nature to all his descendants. If, then, the Son of God became incarnate that He might be the Second Head of our race and infuse a supply of new life into our impoverished nature, does it not follow that our connection with Him must be organic too? How else could we be "members of Christ," as our Catechism says all Christians are? And the Catechism merely follows the still stronger language of S. Paul, who compares the connection between Christ and his members with that between Adam and his wife, who was made "bone of his bone and flesh of his flesh." The baptized, he says, are "limbs of Christ's Body, (growing) out of His flesh and out of His bones." He asserts the same doctrine in another way in his great chapter on the Resurrection of the body. "The first man Adam was made a living soul; the last Adam was made a life-giving (ζωοποιοῦν) spirit. Howbeit that was not first which is spiritual, but that which is natural; and afterward that which is spiritual. The first man is of the earth, earthy: the Second Man is the Lord from heaven. As is the earthy, such are they also that are earthy: and as is the heavenly, such are they also that are heavenly. And as we have borne the image of the earthy, we shall also bear the image of the heavenly." S. Peter does not hesitate to say that Christians are made "partakers of the Divine Nature;" and our Lord Himself conveys the same idea under the image of the Vine and its branches, and still more emphatically in that wonderful Sacramental discourse recorded in the sixth chapter of S. John's Gospel. He calls Himself "the Bread of life," "the living Bread which came down from heaven." And then more plainly, "The Bread that I will give is My Flesh, which I will give for the life of the world." And when His hearers questioned the possibility of such a gift, He repeated His assertion with a solemn asseveration: "Verily, verily I say unto you, Except ye eat the Flesh of the Son of Man, and drink His Blood, ye have no life in you. Whoso eateth My Flesh and drinketh My Blood *hath* eternal life, and I will raise him up at the Last Day."

I dare not explain away these solemn words. I must believe that they contain some deep meaning; for it is incredible that our loving Saviour would have permitted Himself to indulge in misleading rhetoric. He saw that His very strong and solemn language was liable to be misunderstood—that, in fact, it was misunderstood by the bulk of those whom He was addressing. But He had not to think of them alone. **Numberless generations yet unborn were in His thought, in** whose ears those words would sound as the glad tidings of a life from the dead. Like His own Incarnation, it was the **lot of the doctrine on which He was insisting to be "set for the fall and rising again of many in Israel, and for a sign which should be spoken against."** But not one jot or tittle of that doctrine would He explain away. Rather than **do so He was** willing to risk not merely the desertion of the offended multitude but of His own small band of disciples. **"Will ye also go away?"** They did not, for they acknowledged that His words were "the words of eternal life." But the question clearly implies that He would have preferred their forsaking Him to the alternative of watering down the "hard saying" which had offended and repelled the multitude.

With such an example before me I dare not trifle with our Lord's emphatic **words.** I will not presume to say that they are metaphorical, seeing that Himself pointedly declined to admit any such interpretation of them when the people of Capernaum challenged them. But if not metaphorical, **what are they?** Our reason revolts against their apparent meaning, **and we may be** tempted to ask, with the puzzled multitude,—"How can this man give us His flesh to eat?" Our Lord Himself has supplied the answer. His words were true, and had a most real meaning. But they were not to be understood in any gross materialistic sense. " It is the spirit that quickeneth; the flesh profiteth nothing. The words that I speak unto you, they are spirit and they are life." In other words, when He spoke of giving His Flesh and Blood as the food of His people, He did not mean by flesh and blood anything that the bodily senses could apprehend or a chemist could analyze into its elements. In that sense our Lord's Flesh and Blood are certainly not present either in the Eucharist or elsewhere. It is true that He called on His disciples to testify to the reality of His "Flesh and Bones" after His Resurrection. True also, that the Fourth Article asserts that "Christ did truly rise again from death, and took again His Body, with flesh, bones, and all things pertaining to the perfection of man's nature; wherewith He ascended into Heaven, and there sitteth until He return to judge all men at the Last Day." But it is evident that whatever is meant by the Flesh and Bones of our Lord's Resurrection Body they are generically different from our flesh and bones. What we call flesh and bone is simply a consolidation of certain gases which may be resolved into their original elements; and then they cease to be flesh and bone. But while they remain flesh and bone they are subject to decay, and the ceaseless waste of tissue requires to be repaired by the assimilation of congenial nutriment.

Therefore, a body of such flesh and bone as we have any experience of cannot subsist without food; nor can it pass through material substances, such as a closed door, nor mount up into the air contrary to the law of gravity, nor become visible and invisible without apparent cause. But our Lord's Body did all this. It is incorruptible, and therefore needs no food. It passed repeatedly through a closed door.* It ascended through the air in a manner contrary to all the known properties of a human body. It appeared suddenly, and as suddenly vanished out of sight. Even before His Resurrection our Lord's Body appears to have possessed properties which ours do not possess, or possess only in germ. He walked upon the waves, and gave Peter

---

* Dr. Vogan ('The Doctrine of the Eucharist,' pp. 558-560) denies this. He admits that our Lord's sudden appearance, "the doors being shut," and His sudden invisibility, were miraculous; but he maintains that in each case the subject of the miracle was not our Lord's Body, but in the first case the material substance of wood, and in the other the circumambient air. "We can suppose that by His divine power the doors opened of their own accord for his admission." "A body will disappear to one if the rays of light from it be intercepted, or if he will even close his eyes. And He who could 'still the raging of the sea' could also change or suspend the properties of the air, so as to prevent his person from being seen through it." That is to say, instead of our Lord's Body being supernatural, and therefore independent of the laws of matter, He possessed some talismanic Sesame which could open closed doors and close the open eyes of the multitude. By a parity of reasoning, Dr. Vogan would hold that our Lord ascended from Mount Olivet in an etherial balloon. I do not consider it necessary, nor would it be reverent, to discuss puerilities of reasoning like this.

power to do so till his faith failed him. He made Himself invisible on more than one occasion when His enemies were about to seize Him; and He was transfigured on Mount Tabor. This seems to show that His Body was in Its essence always a spiritual body. So that It could be emancipated at will from the laws of matter, and could retire within the sphere of spiritual laws. Of course His absolute sinlessness, and the union of His Sacred Humanity with His Divine Person, must always have made a certain difference between His Body and those of ordinary men. But sin, with its consequences, does not belong to the integrity of human nature, though it suppresses the natural development of our bodies, so that they cannot realize their perfection without the violent dissolution which we call Death. But surely the properties of the spiritual body are even now latent in our mortal frame, and, but for sin, might show themselves independent of the laws of matter, as our Lord's Body did occasionally before His Resurrection, and normally after that event.

When, therefore, the Fourth Article affirms that "Christ did truly rise again from death, and took again His Body, with flesh, bones, and all things pertaining to the perfection of man's nature, wherewith He ascended into Heaven," it does not at all follow that the phrase, "His body, with flesh and bones," connotes the same thing as it does in the case of our bodies. In fact, it cannot do so; for "flesh and blood cannot inherit the kingdom of God, neither doth corruption inherit incorruption." Our Lord's Body possesses, of course, "all things pertaining to the perfection of man's nature." But it is certain that flesh and blood, bone and muscle, do not belong "to the perfection of man's nature." They belong to the region of decay and death, and therefore our Lord has them not. The terms may express the nearest approach which our minds can now make to the conception of a spiritual body; but they cannot be pressed literally without violence both to Holy Scripture and to right reason.

What, then, did our Lord mean by saying that He would give His Flesh and Blood for the food of His people? I admit that His words were, in a sense, figurative; but they were figurative only in the sense in which all human language is figurative when it attempts to deal with the realities of the spiritual world. They were figurative because they expressed less, not because they expressed more, than He intended to convey. "It is the spirit that quickeneth; the flesh profiteth nothing. The words that I speak unto you, they are spirit and they are life." That is to say, even in material things it is not the gross mass of material particles that "profiteth," but that inner essence which is too subtle for the apprehension of the senses, and which eludes all the skill of science. A chemist can take any organized body, from that of a man to that of an acorn, and separate it into its component parts; but the principle of life escapes in the process, and he cannot restore it with all his science. He can make, unmake, and remake a crystal; but he cannot make a blade of grass, nor restore its vitality when it has fled. The lisping infant knows why a blade of grass grows just as well as the wisest philosopher. "It is the spirit that quickeneth." All things that live have their root in a spiritual cause, and that cause, in its last analysis, is God. "In Him we live, and move, and have our being," and apart from Him there can be no life. In this sense the whole universe of life may be said to feed upon its God, and it is a glimpse of this truth which has given such vitality to Pantheism through all its manifold phases.

Taking our Lord's explanation, therefore, together with the " hard saying," of which the people of Capernaum complained, it is easy enough to understand, though not easy to comprehend, the doctrine which He taught. By "flesh and blood" He meant His real substantial humanity. In Baptism we are "born again," as He explained to Nicodemus; we are made " members of Christ "—that is, we are brought into organic connection with His sinless humanity. And that connection is supernaturally maintained through the channel of the Holy Eucharist. Other ordinances bring us within the influences of His grace; this places our humanity in actual contact with His, so that virtue goes out of It to feed us and gradually " transform our vile bodies, so that **they may** be fashioned **like** unto His glorious Body."*

It is no answer to this doctrine to say that **it encourages** "Sacerdotalism," **and** implies the existence of a class of men dealing in "magical rites" and endowed to work "invisible miracles." As a matter of fact, it is not a bit more wonderful that the Second Adam should transmit His humanity to His members by means of two Sacraments than that the First Adam should pass on his humanity to his descendants through the instrumentality of two parents. The one is just as much an "invisible miracle" as the other. They are equally beyond the ken of human intellect, and they are equally reasonable.

But it is asked: How is it possible that our Lord's Body can be present at one and the same moment on ten thousand different altars? "For though a spirit is so much more subtile than a material body; and a body, supposed to move like a spirit, may also **be** supposed **to** have inconceivable rapidity of motion, and the power of intimate penetration into and under other substances; yet no finite body can, in its very substance, be in more places than one at the same time. If it can, why not in many places? Why not everywhere? And so the finite would be, not finite, but infinite."†

It would be just as reasonable to ask: How is it

* See Appendix, Note B.
† Dr. Vogan on 'The True Doctrine of the Eucharist,' **p. 561.**

possible that the flesh and blood of a man living in Australia should be present in his children here in London? As a matter of fact, Adam's flesh and blood, that is, his essential humanity, is present really and substantially in **all** the millions of his descendants. And shall we declare that to be impossible to God the Son which is an admitted fact in the case of the fallen Adam? Shall the First Adam be capable of disseminating his perverted nature among all the human beings who have come out of his loins? And shall the Second Adam be incapable of imparting His life-giving Humanity to the members of His body?

But the plain truth is, Dr. Vogan **and those** who agree with him do not understand the doctrine which they controvert. Like the inhabitants of Capernaum, they seem unable to lift their minds out of the slough **of** naturalism, and they suppose accordingly that when we speak of the Real Presence of our Lord's Body in the Sacrament we mean the presence of so many cubic inches of ponderable matter. Can they not see that **even** their own bodies do not consist, after all, of the **gross mass** of material particles which sight and touch can apprehend. These **are in** a state of perpetual flux, passing away with every respiration, and entering into **new** combinations. So that literally we have not the same body from hour **to** hour, viewed on its material side. Underlying this material covering, however, **is** an informing **substance** which remains unchanged, and which is able to multiply itself indefinitely through the process of natural generation. But our Lord's Body is not a natural body, and does not belong to the natural, but to the supernatural, order of things. He came to create us anew, to place our poverty-stricken nature in communication with His own vivifying Humanity, so that a new life might circulate through our frame, and make us " new creatures." The Sacraments are thus the "continuation of the Incarnation," as I think Moehler calls them; they are the channels through which the nature of the Second Head of our race is conveyed to His members. I know of no other way, for Holy Scripture reveals none, in which we can be made partakers of Christ. Faith is of course necessary; but faith is useless if we refuse to use the means. Naaman's faith led him all the way to the Prophet of Israel; but if he had acted on his first impulse and refused to "wash seven times in Jordan," what would his faith have availed him? And just as little will faith now avail the Christian who prefers the Abana and Pharpar of his own devices to the one simple way which the wisdom of God has provided for the cure of spiritual leprosy. There was no inherent virtue in the waters of Jordan to heal the leper any more than in the "rivers of Damascus." But God had chosen to energize through the one and not through the other; and that made all the difference. So now: there is no virtue in water or in bread and wine to heal the sinner of his hereditary malady. But if God has chosen, for the trial of our faith, to make those "beggarly elements" the channels of His grace, have we any right to reject the channels and still expect the grace? To my mind it does not appear at all more wonderful that bread and wine should, under God's appointment, be able to sustain our spiritual nature, than that bread and wine should be able to sustain our physical nature. Of themselves they could do neither; as the channels through which His power acts they can, with equal facility, do both.

The fact is, the popular prejudice against the Sacramental system, while ostensibly based on a jealous desire to exalt God's power, springs in reality from a contracted view of His power. "Every good gift and every perfect gift," alike in the kingdom of nature and of grace, "is from above, and cometh down from the Father of lights, with whom is no variableness, neither shadow of turning." But every one of these gifts reaches us through the intervention of some intermediate causation. A bountiful harvest is as much the fruit of God's grace as purity of heart. In the one case God energizes through the operation of rain, and sunshine, and human toil. Why should it be derogatory to His power to suppose that in the other case also it should energize through the agency of material instrumentality and human co-operation? "So long as its Sacramental principle remains," says an able and cultivated writer, "the Established Church rests upon a theory of religion utterly at variance with all the residuary varieties of Puritan faith, and amounting, as many of us conceive, to a reversal of the very essence of Christianity, for it intercepts that *immediateness of relation* between the human spirit and the Divine which is the distinctive boon of Jesus to the world, and it reinstates that resort to *mediation*, 'and channels of grace,' and magically-endowed men, which it was His special aim to sweep away and render impossible."* This objection tells quite as much against man's physical organization as it does against the "Sacramental principle." There is no "immediateness of relation" that we know of "between the human spirit and the Divine." As at present constituted, Mr. Martineau's spirit holds relation to the Divine, not immediately, but mediately through the material organ of the brain, which again is sustained in its active vitality by constant supplies of earthly food. And is Mr. Martineau so very sure that he, too, does not "resort to mediation, and channels of grace"? What, then, are the books or discourses which instruct his intellect, the friends who kindle his affections, the sights and sounds which delight his imagination? What are these, and all the other innumerable influences which act beneficially on the soul of man, and lift it up in thankfulness and adoration to its God, but instances, in their own way, of that very "Sacramental principle"

* 'Why Dissent?' By James Martineau, p. 14.

which is thoughtlessly supposed to be "a reversal of the very essence of Christianity?" And as to "magically-endowed men," has it never happened to Mr. Martineau to meet any such? Does he know none of his acquaintance who possesses a magic influence, a subtle indescribable charm which he finds it hard to resist? And whence is that influence derived? Is its origin in man? Or does it not, like all things good and beautiful, come from God? Is it not a fact that God does give to some men gifts which He denies to others?—external gifts of wealth, social rank, and the like; personal gifts, whether of physical beauty or of intellectual or moral endowments. And is it not true that by means of such gifts their possessors have a power of influencing their fellows for good or evil which others do not enjoy? Why does Mr. Martineau encourage people to attend his place of worship and listen to his eloquent sermons? Do not his voice, his words, his thoughts, "reinstate that resort to mediation . . . and magically-endowed men, which," he tells us, "it was His (Christ's) special aim to sweep away and render impossible"? What is an eloquent preacher but a mediator "between the human spirit and the Divine"?

The truth is, all this declamation about "the difference between a sacerdotal and a personal Christianity" is pure unmitigated rant. I am far from saying that all who indulge in it are conscious of the utter hollowness of their reasoning. My complaint is, that they are *not* aware of it. They use a traditional phraseology, which they do not take the trouble to understand, otherwise they would see that this theory of a *personal* as opposed to a *sacerdotal* Christianity leads to isolation and selfishness, and finds its natural expression in the question of the first murderer, "**Am** I my brother's keeper?"

What, then, are the ideas which lie at the root of what is called Sacerdotalism? Speaking broadly, they **are two in** number: first, a recognition of man's unworthiness to approach God; secondly, his need of some check to counteract the innate selfishness of our nature.

(1.) We are all intended, laity as well as clergy, to be "kings and priests unto God." If man had never fallen there would have been no need of a special priesthood. All would have been equally worthy to offer an acceptable service to their Maker, as all will be hereafter in Heaven. This is the ideal towards which we are to strive, and to help us to realize our own unworthiness it has pleased God to ordain an order of men, personally as unworthy as the rest, to be "ministers and stewards of his mysteries," or, as St. Paul elsewhere calls them, "ambassadors" between men and God. It is remarkable that the immediate cause of the appointment of the Aaronic priesthood seems to have been the public acknowledgment of unworthiness made by the general congregation. The circumstance is related as follows by Moses:—

"And it came to pass when ye heard the voice out of

the midst of the darkness (for the mountain did burn with fire), that ye came near unto me, even all the heads of your tribes, and your elders; and ye said, Behold, the Lord our God hath shown us His glory and His greatness, and we have heard His voice out of the midst of the fire: we have seen this day that God doth talk with man, and he liveth. Now therefore why should we die? for this great fire will consume us: if we hear the voice of the Lord our God any more, then we shall die. For who is there of all flesh that hath heard the voice of the living God speaking out of the midst of the fire, as we have, and lived? Go thou near, and hear all that the Lord our God shall say: and speak thou unto us all that the Lord our God shall speak unto thee; and we will hear it and do it. And the Lord heard the voice of your words, when ye spake unto me; and the Lord said unto me, I have heard the voice of the words of this people, which they have spoken unto thee: they have well said all that they have spoken."

Accordingly Aaron and his sons were consecrated to the office of the priesthood soon after this incident, and they **became** the appointed mediators between Jehovah and the general congregation. Still the people were not suffered **to** rest in this as a final and unchangeable arrangement. Their true ideal was always kept before **them.** They were reminded that, in spite of the Aaronic priesthood, they still continued ideally " a kingdom of priests, a holy nation." They were unworthy now to realize that ideal; but they were to rest satisfied with nothing short of it. And St. Peter, in like manner and for the same reason, addresses the Christians of his day as "a royal priesthood;" while St. John saw the ideal fulfilled when he heard the saints in bliss giving thanks for having been made "kings and priests unto God."

(2.) But, secondly, man needs something to counteract the inborn tendency of his nature to become selfish, to think of himself too much, and of others too little. Now the notion of a *personal* as opposed to a *sacerdotal* Christianity is a notion which is thoroughly selfish, and therefore anti-Christian. For it implies that human beings are a mere aggregate of unconnected units, each complete in itself, and striving after its own perfection. And I can conceive nothing better calculated to foster this view than the doctrine that every man is to depend entirely on himself, neither needing nor receiving any help from his fellows. Mr. Martineau's premisses—and they are also the premisses of a theological school in our Church—would logically lead not only to the abolition of a special priesthood, but of all intercessory prayer whatever.

The teaching of Christianity, on the contrary, is that human beings are essentially one family—"the whole family in heaven and in earth." And to impress this truth upon us God has made us necessary to each other. On the right hand and on the left, from the cradle to the grave, we need **the help of others.** Relationships of all kinds and degrees branch out in all directions and enclose us in a complicated network of innumerable sympathies. Can anything be more certain than that God has made us the guardians of each other's eternal welfare? Cannot parents train their children in such a way as to ruin them everlastingly? Cannot all of us, men or women, priests or laymen, use any talent that God may have entrusted to our keeping in saving or in ruining the souls which come within the circle of our influence? What is there in the doctrine of Sacerdotalism that approaches this in mystery? The Church of England claims for her priesthood the power of absolving penitents. But this is an official, not a personal, power. It has no effect if used against God's will; and its efficacy depends, after all, on the state of the heart to which it is applied. But beauty of person, and charm of manner, and brilliancy of intellect and the like, are personal gifts, and may be used to the ruin of our neighbour against the will and intention of the Almighty Giver. What is there in the doctrine of Sacerdotalism so terrible and inexplicable as this? Is it not a patent fact that we all stand in a kind of sacerdotal relation to each other? And is the doctrine of the Christian priesthood anything else but one department of a system which pervades and governs the entire sphere of man's life on earth?

It is, of course, natural enough, and, in fact, inevitable, that one who does not believe in the Trinity and Incarnation should reject the "Sacramental principle," since that principle means the perpetuation of the Incarnation. But surely nothing but an unreasoning prejudice could prevent any intelligent believer in the Incarnation from seeing that the Sacramental System is its natural complement. In the minds of a number of people who sincerely believe in the Divinity of Christ the Incarnation is regarded as an historical event that took place some eighteen centuries ago, and whose interest for us is practically bounded by the Sacrifice on Calvary. According to this view Christianity is absorbed in the Atonement, and the Atonement is not regarded as a process going on continually in its application to us, but as a past fact consummated once for all on the Cross, and having no direct relation to our life except in the way of having appeased an angry God, and therefore supplied a motive for lively gratitude on our parts. Accordingly, in the Holy Communion no positive gift is supposed to be imparted. The Sacrament is only a symbolical picture of the death of Christ, well calculated to bring that event vividly before us, and to stir up grateful emotions in our hearts in consequence. But the God-Man is absent—far away beyond Sirius and the Milky Way; and we are to ascend where He is in imagination and feeling. And this is what is called the " spiritual presence" of Christ in the Holy Communion, or rather in the heart of the worthy communicant. It is manifestly no presence at **all.** It is as if a man should think that he was spiritually present in India by dwelling in thought on a loved brother who happened to live there. In truth, the reality of our Lord's Humanity as subsisting and energizing now has gradually and silently dropped out of the practical belief of a great many among us. Their gaze is ever backward, and they live in the memory of the past rather than in the enjoyment of the present. This explains why Ascension Day, which testifies to Christ's continued Humanity, has fallen into disuse among those who reject the Sacramental System.

All this is a grave misconception of the central idea of Christianity. We are not to regard Christ as an historical character belonging to the past, but as a **present** Person out of whose life-giving Humanity virtue is continually going out for the healing of the nations. Human nature, viewed in the abstract, fell when Adam sinned; but his descendants were made partakers of the Fall by their organic connection with the first parent. **In like** manner, humanity, viewed in the lump, was **saved** when Christ triumphed over sin and death. But the individual members of the race cannot be partakers **of that** salvation except by organic connection with Christ. It **was** no mere gazing on the aboriginal calamity of Eden that has involved us in the consequences of that calamity, nor is it by any mental gazing on the crucifixion of Calvary that we can be regenerated.

The Human Nature of Christ must be communicated to us as literally as the nature of **Adam, else** we have no part or inheritance in the God-Man. Adam is present in all of us, truly, really, and substantially; and if the Second Adam is not present in as real a sense we are not yet redeemed. But there is this difference. **The** *nature* of Adam is literally present in all of us, but not his person: **that** is incommunicable, and being finite it is limited and circumscribed **in** space. Our Lord's Personality, on the other hand, resides **in His** Divine Nature, and that is everywhere. **So** that He is Personally present, and necessarily so, wherever **His** Humanity is present.

Evangelical theology seems to me to be sadly wanting in breadth and depth. It is apt to take a low mechanical view of the great facts of Christianity and **to** fasten down their significance to what logicians call their "inseparable accidents." It practically regards the Sacrifice of Christ as beginning and ending on **Calvary.** What a poor notion such a view gives of the love **and** condescension of our Incarnate Lord! To us, with our limited vision and sense of guilt, death appears a great calamity. **It puts an end to all our** plans, tears us from a thousand endearing associations, and **dismisses** us to an unknown world **and** an uncertain destiny. **To** Him death was but a temporal incident **in** a life-long sacrifice. He "drank of **the** brook **in the way,"** and passed behind the veil to offer Himself **as a** " perpetual sacrifice."* The essence of self-sacrifice is in the consent of the will. That once accomplished, the sacrifice is complete so far as the sufferer is concerned, though circumstances may require its consummation in the death of the victim. Abraham's self-sacrifice was complete when, in obedience to the Divine command, **he** raised his arm to strike his child; and the Church has always conceded the crown of martyrdom to those whose martyrdom was only in will. God has been sacrificing Himself from eternity. **He is** self-sufficient, absolutely perfect in the eternal harmony of **a** threefold Personality in an indivisible Substance. He needs nothing from without, and **the created** universe, therefore, with all its joyous sights and sounds, is but the overflowing of an infinite love which delights to share its blessedness. To Him this perpetual self-sacrifice involves no pain because His love is perfect, and therefore "hath" no "torment." But when the eternal Son laid aside His manifold perfections, and circumscribed His infinitude by the imperfections of humanity, the pain that is latent in the love of all finite natures—the pain of unsatisfied yearning—became manifest "in strong crying and tears."†

---

* Both **the** argument and the sense seem to require that εἰς τὸ διηνεκὲς, in Heb. x. 12, should be connected with προσενέγκας.

†   "The best of men
That e'er wore earth about Him was a sufferer—
A soft, meek, patient, humble, tranquil spirit—
The first true gentleman that ever breathed."—*Dekker.*

He felt the outpourings of His self-sacrifice repelled on all sides by the sins of men, and driven back upon their source. "He could do no mighty work there because of their unbelief," and His human soul felt the pangs of baffled love.

In self-sacrifice, therefore, lies the happiness of God. And this self-sacrifice is eternal; first, in the relations of the Persons of the Blessed Trinity to each other, and then in the sphere of created life. In self-sacrifice lies our happiness also, if we only knew it. "Whosoever will save his life shall lose it; and whosoever will lose his life for My sake shall find it." We must therefore somehow be partakers of Christ's sufferings. We must be brought *en rapport* with his enduring sacrifice; and if we are to credit the testimony of Christian antiquity the Holy Eucharist is the means by which this is effected. Whatever we may think of the doctrines of the Real Presence and of the Eucharistic Sacrifice, it is the plainest matter of fact that they are the doctrines of the ancient Liturgies and the early Fathers. It would be easy to prove this; but it would require too long a digression from my immediate subject. Let one passage suffice therefore by way of specimen. "Be diligent therefore," says St. Ignatius, "to make use of the one Eucharist; for there is one Flesh of our Lord Jesus Christ, and one chalice (for bringing us) into union with His Blood, and one altar, as also one Bishop, with the Presbyters and Deacons, my fellow-servants; so that whatever ye do, ye may do it according to the will of God."*

This testimony, be it remarked, is from a martyred Saint who lived early enough to have conversed with the Apostles. It possesses a value, therefore, only second to that of Holy Scripture, and it seems to me to prove these two things: first, that the Real Presence and the Eucharistic sacrifice were then among the undisputed doctrines of the Christian Church; secondly, that the ecclesiastical hierarchy then consisted of the three orders of Bishop, Presbyter, and Deacon. Ignatius does not argue in favour of either; he simply appeals to them as admitted facts. But while insisting on this, I feel bound, at the same time, to express my opinion that no small part of the prejudice against these doctrines arises from the incautious advocacy of some High Churchmen, who are prone to use exaggerated language without taking any pains to explain their meaning. And this is true especially of the doctrine of our Lord's Real Presence in the Sacrament of the Holy Communion.

Of course He is present to those only who have faith —that is to say, they only can "discern" Him. Others may come in contact with Him, but they know it not. Blind men do not "discern" the light of the sun; but it is there for all that. Its existence is an objective reality independent alike of the vision and blindness of those on whom it shines. And so, in the Holy Com-

* Epist. ad. Philad., ch. iv.

munion, the faith of the communicant has absolutely nothing to do with the Presence of Christ. Faith creates nothing; its province is to receive some gift already existing independently of it. If it were not so, it would follow that when all the communicants happened to be without faith, a contingency by no means improbable, there would be no Sacrament at all. What the doctrine of our Lord's real objective Presence in the Sacrament, independently of the faith of the recipient, means is simply this: that the virtue of the Sacrament is rooted in a cause external to man. To insist, therefore, on an exclusively subjective Presence is, in reality, to be a Pelagian. It is a curious "Nemesis of faith" that those who began by decrying human nature as utterly depraved, and denouncing good works as "filthy rags," should end by ascribing to an act of man the whole credit and merit of human salvation. Not by Divinely ordained Sacraments, not by any real participation in Christ's Humanity, not by anything external to himself, is man saved, but by faith, which is an internal act of his own soul. And so depraved humanity, after all, is able to save itself! How different is such a doctrine from that of those who accept the Sacramental principle! for the essence of Sacramentalism lies in believing that everything beautiful and good and true comes from God, but almost invariably through intermediate, and generally material, agency. So that the whole material creation is one vast veil of Sacramentalism behind which "the Father worketh hitherto" through all the forms of animated existence, from a daisy to an archangel.*

But what has all this to do with the Athanasian Creed? Very much, as I humbly venture to think. For the attack on the Athanasian Creed is in reality an attack on the doctrines of the Trinity and the Incarnation. Of course I do not mean to say that those who make the attack intend it in that sense. I know well that most of them would repel any such insinuation with just indignation; and I have not the least doubt that they sincerely regard the Athanasian Creed as a dangerous outpost, the abolition of which would strengthen rather than weaken the bulwarks of the Faith. I am quite sure that their intentions are admirable. I am equally sure that their policy is thoroughly mischievous, and that its success would be disastrous to the faith, and therefore to the morals, of the people of England. It is possible that no very marked change would take place in your lifetime or in mine. But the reverse is also possible; and, in any case, man does not live for himself alone, or for his own generation alone. It is the duty of everyone, however humble his position or abilities may be, to do what he can for God and His truth before he is summoned hence. One of the most ignoble sayings ever dictated by a selfish love of ease was that of the amiable Hezekiah when he heard of the

* See Appendix, Note C.

impending ruin of his country, for which he was partly responsible:—" Is it not good if there be peace and truth in my days?"

Now I am not content that there should be "peace and truth in my days" only, even if I were sure of that; which I am not. It is the bounden duty of us all to hand on the lamp of truth to our successors without any diminution of the sacred flame; and for my own part—I say it with all humility—I would rather lay down the commission which I received from the Church of England than be a party to the abolition or mutilation of a Creed which has been a source of innumerable blessings to myself, and also, I venture to say, to many of those who have lifted up their heel against it, though they may not be conscious of their obligations. The Athanasian Creed is attacked because it is alleged to be "heretical" and uncharitable. Let it be surrendered in answer to that indictment, and what follows? That all those passages in Holy Scripture which are identical in principle with the "damnatory clauses" must be given up as "barbarian curses," excusable perhaps in the darkness of a rude and ignorant age, but quite unsuitable to our enlightened ideas. More than one speaker in Convocation met this objection by the astounding plea, that denunciations which are right and proper in the Bible are quite unjustifiable in a human composition. I call this distinction astounding because it is not only degrading to the Bible, but fatal to the first

M

principles of morality. For it means, in plain English, that the Bible may have one kind of morality, and the creeds of Christendom quite another. I refuse to believe anything so monstrous. No one shall persuade me that propositions which are "uncharitable," "untrue," and "barbarous" in the Athanasian Creed can be other than "uncharitable," "untrue," and "barbarous" in the Bible. Either the "damnatory clauses" of the Athanasian Creed are reasonable and just, or those of the New Testament are not. There is no escape from that conclusion. And it is a very serious one. For if the Athanasian Creed is unfit for congregational use on account of its "damnatory clauses," it follows that we must have an expurgated edition of the Bible for the public services of the Church. Not a single objection can be urged against the "damnatory clauses" of the Athanasian Creed which does not apply with equal force against the "damnatory clauses" which are scattered plentifully up and down the New Testament. I will not dwell on the disputed passage in St. Mark, though Mr. Burgon's work on the subject seems to me to leave its genuineness at least an open question. It is not on an isolated passage here and there in the Bible that the doctrine of the "damnatory clauses" depends; it pervades the whole Gospel message. Both Our Lord Himself and the inspired writers of the New Testament insist on the necessity of a right faith as strongly as they do on the necessity of moral rectitude. I am aware that the Dean of Westminster asserts the contrary. "A Creed," he says, "which asserts in the most emphatic language that, in order to be 'saved' (whatever sense we attach to that word), it is 'before all things necessary to hold the Catholic Faith,' can hardly be said to be in the spirit of Him who declared, 'Not every one that saith unto the Lord, Lord, shall enter into the kingdom of heaven, but he that doeth the will of my Father which is in heaven;' or of His Apostles, who proclaimed, 'In every land he that feareth God and doeth righteousness is accepted of Him;' or, 'circumcision availeth nothing, nor uncircumcision, but the keeping of the commandments of God;' or, 'He that doeth righteousness is righteous.'"

I humbly venture to suggest that these passages are not to the point. If, as I believe, our Blessed Lord has revealed to us certain doctrinal truths which are necessary to salvation, then belief in them is necessarily implied in the texts which the Dean has cited. What warrant have we for supposing that belief in the Catholic Faith is excluded from the obligation to "do the will" of God, and to "keep his commandments?" I know of none, and therefore I shall continue, till better informed, to believe that he who deliberately rejects an article of faith transgresses God's commandments as really and opposes His will as effectually as the man who breaks the moral law.

The Dean admits, indeed, that "other expressions of

another kind may doubtless be found in other parts of the Bible." "Let them be fairly considered," he says. "But they are not **its** key-note, or its general tone. They belong to modes of feeling on their face more or less transitory, more or less exceptional." Is this a correct statement of the facts? Let us see.

"This **is** life eternal," says our Lord, "that they might know Thee, the only true God, and Jesus Christ whom Thou hast sent." Again; when the Jews asked Him, "What shall we do that we may work the works of God?" "Jesus answered and said unto them, "This **is** the work of God that ye believe on Him whom He hath sent." And when He warns evil-doers of the doom that awaits them **He** tells them that "He will appoint them their portion with *the unbelievers*." Here our loving Saviour Himself puts immoral living and pertinacious unbelief on the same level, and He even seems to intimate that unbelief is the more dangerous of the two. The first condition of "doing the works of God" is a right belief as to the doctrine of the Incarnation: "This is the work of God, that ye believe on Him whom He hath sent." Hold that faith in sincerity, and "the works of God" will follow as a natural consequence. Reject it with your eyes open, and you place yourself outside the pale of salvation. For "God so loved the world that He gave His only-begotten Son, that whoso**ever** believeth **in** Him should **not** perish, but have everlasting life. He that believeth on Him is not condemned; but he that believeth not is condemned already, because he hath not believed in the name of the only-begotten Son of God." Nothing can be plainer than this. To forfeit "everlasting life," that is, to "perish," is here declared to be the lot of him who refuses to believe in the doctrine of the Incarnation. So far forth as a man rejects that doctrine he is "condemned already"—that is to say, he has, *ipso facto* placed himself beyond the pale of salvation.

This is our Lord's teaching, and the whole scope of the New Testament confirms it. When the Philippian jailer asked Paul and Silas, "Sirs, what must I do to be saved?" the Apostle replied immediately, "Believe on the Lord Jesus Christ, and thou shalt be saved, and thy house." John the Baptist certainly enjoined "works meet for repentance" on those who flocked to consult him by the banks of Jordan; but he also said, "He that believeth on the Son hath everlasting life; and he that believeth not the Son shall not see life; but the wrath of God abideth on him." "The disciple whom Jesus loved" is equally urgent as to the necessity of a true faith. "Whosoever denieth the Son, the same hath not the Father." And again; "He that hath the Son hath life; and he that hath not the Son of God hath not life." Not to have life is to "perish," and therefore perdition is declared by St. John to be the inevitable doom of those who reject the doctrine of the Incarnation. And he deemed this truth so paramount that it was the principal motive of his writing his Epistle. "These things have I written unto you that believe on the **name of** the Son of God, that ye may know that ye have eternal life, and that ye may believe on the name of the Son of God." Again: "Every spirit that confesseth that Jesus Christ is come in the flesh is of God. But every spirit that confesseth not that Jesus Christ is come in the flesh is not of God." Again: "Many deceivers are entered into the world, who confess not that Jesus Christ is come in the flesh: this is a deceiver and an antichrist." **Once** more: "Look to yourselves, that ye lose **not** those things which ye have wrought; but that ye receive a full reward. Whoever transgresseth and abideth not in the doctrine of Christ hath not God. He that abideth in the doctrine of Christ, he hath both the Father and the Son." To the same purport is St. Peter's denunciation of those "false teachers" "who privily shall bring in damnable heresies, even denying the Lord that bought them, and bring upon themselves swift destruction. And many shall follow their pernicious ways ($\tau\alpha\hat{\iota}\varsigma\ \dot{\alpha}\pi\omega\lambda\epsilon\dot{\iota}\alpha\iota\varsigma$); by reason of whom the way of truth shall be blasphemed." Here the denial of the Incarnation is said to be a "damnable heresy" ($\alpha\dot{\iota}\rho\dot{\epsilon}\sigma\epsilon\iota\varsigma\ \dot{\alpha}\pi\omega\lambda\epsilon\dot{\iota}\alpha\varsigma$), leading to "swift destruction." And **the** same doctrine is taught by the Apostle as the direct inspiration of the Pentecostal gift. Immediately after the outpouring of Pentecost he told the Jews that in "**the name of Jesus Christ** of Nazareth alone" was salvation to be found: "for there is none other name under heaven given among men whereby we must be saved." Will anyone tell me the difference between this Apostolic doctrine and the much-abused proposition of the Athanasian Creed: "Which Faith except every one do keep whole and undefiled, without doubt he shall perish everlastingly"? The large-hearted St. Paul, too, who was willing to be "accursed" for the sake of his people, tells us that "all" are to be "damned who believe not the truth, but have pleasure in unrighteousness;" that is to say, the deliberate rejection of the truth is in itself unrighteousness. There could not be a stronger assertion of the immorality of unbelief. And, as I have noticed above, "the unbelievers" are reckoned by St. John among those who "shall have their part in the lake which burneth with fire and brimstone; which is the Second Death." "Antichrists," "liars," "false prophets," "deceivers," "seducers," "grievous wolves,"—such are the terms in which heretics are described by our Lord and His Apostles; one of whom—he who is emphatically called "the disciple whom Jesus loved"—does not hesitate to say that the sacred rites of hospitality ought religiously to be denied to him who impugns the doctrine of the Incarnation. "If there come any unto you," he says, "and bring not this doctrine, receive him not into your house, neither bid him God-speed; for he that biddeth him God-speed is partaker of his evil deeds."

To my mind these passages—and I have by no means exhausted all that might be quoted in the same strain—are absolutely identical in meaning with the "damnatory clauses" of the Athanasian Creed. They must all alike be understood with the qualifications which common sense suggests, and on which I have dilated to some extent already; or they must all alike be condemned and abolished. There is no other alternative. And therefore let the assailants of the Athanasian Creed look to it. They are putting a weapon in the hands of unbelief wherewith to destroy the authority of that Book which they all profess to revere. The statements which they denounce with such vehement thoughtlessness belong to the very essence of the Gospel and are an integral part of Christianity; and I hold therefore that the Athanasian Creed and Christianity must logically stand or fall together. It is no answer to this to say that, as a matter of fact, the practical disuse of the Athanasian Creed in the Roman Church has inflicted no injury on the Faith. For I should be disposed, in the first place, to question the matter of fact. I have travelled a good deal in Italy, and I never heard the Athanasian Creed used but once in what might be called congregational worship. But I am bound to add that I have seldom met with an educated Italian layman who could be said to have a firm hold on the fundamental doctrines of Christianity; while a vast number are, under a show of outward conformity, practically unbelievers. I do not undertake to say that this religious indifference, which is so painful a feature of Italian life, is necessarily traceable to the virtual abolition of the Athanasian Creed. But the facts are certainly coincident; and I have no doubt that the withdrawal of the Athanasian Creed from the cognizance of the laity, and the substitution of less edifying *credenda* in its place, have been among the disintegrating forces which have brought about the present religious condition of Italy. But, in the second place, the Athanasian Creed has never been denounced in the Church of Rome. It has been gradually displaced; but no indignity has ever been put upon it. And therefore its disuse does not react injuriously on the Bible. But to give it up deliberately and in the face of day as an uncharitable document which teaches doctrines "avowedly heretical," or "savouring of heresy," is to give up the very kernel of the Gospel. There is not a single proposition in the Athanasian Creed of which the rejection does not involve the rejection of Christianity. I make that assertion without the least hesitation, and I challenge all the gainsayers of the Creed to disprove it. Of course a person may from prejudice, or ignorance, or confusion of thought, or some other cause, be unable to embrace some of the propositions of the Creed, and yet remain all the while a good Christian. It is none the less true, however, that all the propositions of the Creed hang together, and that the rejection of any one of them would strike Christianity to the heart. The Dean of Westminster takes a different view; and he has displayed much ingenuity in tracing out the various significations which have at different times attached to the word "person." But what then? The word person has at last settled down into a definite meaning, and what matters it that it meant at one time a character on the stage or the mask of an actor? Has the word "parson" no definite and legal meaning because it is simply a form of the word "person," and meant originally the same thing? Or what would a judge think of the ingenuity of an advocate who should endeavour to evade the recognized meaning of the word "pulpit" by arguing that it meant originally a theatrical stage? Would he not tell him that the argument was perfectly true as an historical dissertation, but not a bit to the point?

The fact is, many of us are listless about the necessity of maintaining the Faith in its integrity because we are not conscious of the innumerable evils from which it rescued us. The inspired writers of the New Testament lived in the midst of all the nameless abominations and cruelties which a false faith had brought upon our race; and therefore they saw, with a vividness which we cannot realize, that a true Faith was the necessary correlative of a moral life, and was therefore a matter of life and death to mankind. Hence their vehement denunciation of false doctrine and false teachers.

Is the danger quite past? Is morality safe without the safeguard of the Creeds? Have we become so enlightened that we can afford to do without Christianity? Some clever people seem to think so. They point to Unitarians and Pantheists whose virtuous lives put to shame the vaunted orthodoxy of Christians. But the argument is founded on a fallacy. For the fact is, that, born as we are in a Christian land, and surrounded by Christian associations, we cannot conceive what the moral life of man would be apart from the ideas and graces which Christianity has planted in the world. Christianity is in the air, and those who avowedly refuse their allegiance to it talk, nevertheless, in Christian language, use Christian symbols, in some cases avail themselves of Christian rites, and act on the principles of Christian morals. The influences of the Christian Religion are about us like the atmosphere pressing down the evil of our nature on all sides, but so imperceptibly that we are not conscious of it. Philosophers tell us that the air we breathe is impregnated with countless millions of life-germs which we imbibe with every inspiration, and any one of which has the power of reproducing itself speedily and indefinitely throughout our system. Similar to this is the all-pervading presence of Christianity in a Christian land. It is not its votaries merely who receive of its benefits: they are, in a measure, shared alike by believers and unbelievers. All alike draw their moral life from Christian sources, repose on Christian sympathies, appeal to Christian laws. And therefore when any eminent writer, who happens to teach a sound morality while rejecting the Christian Faith, is adduced to prove that morality may exist apart from Christianity, I reply that in the instances produced it does *not* exist apart from Christianity. Not an unbelieving writer can be named, from Rousseau and Voltaire down to the latest German sceptic, who has not purloined all that is good in his writings from Christianity.

But I may be supposed to be a prejudiced advocate. Very good. I appeal to an advocate whose prejudices are all the other way; I mean Mr. James Martineau, one of the most eminent Unitarians of the day. In a letter which he wrote and published thirteen years ago, and which is printed *in extenso* in 'Strictures on the Rev. James Martineau's Letter on the Unitarian Position, by the Rev. R. Brook Aspland,' Mr. Martineau makes the following remarkable confession:—" I am constrained to say that neither my intellectual nor my moral admiration goes heartily with the Unitarian heroes, sects, or productions of any age. Ebionites, Arians, Socinians, all seem to me to contrast unfavourably with their opponents, and to exhibit a type of thought and character far less worthy, on the whole, of the true genius of Christianity. *I am conscious that my deepest obligations, as a learner from others,* **are in almost every department to writers not of my own Creed.** In philosophy I had to unlearn most that I had imbibed from my early text-books and the authors in chief favour with them. In Biblical Interpretation I derive from Calvin and Whitby the help that fails me in Crell and Belsham. In Devotional Literature and Religious Thought I find nothing of ours that does not pale before Augustine, Tauler, and Pascal. And in the poetry of the Church it is the Latin or the German hymns, or the lines of Charles Wesley, or of Keble, that fasten on my memory and heart, and make all else seem poor and cold. I cannot help this. I can only say, I am sure it is no perversity; and I believe the preference is founded in reason and nature, and is already widely spread amongst us. A man's 'Church' must be the home of whatever he most deeply loves, trusts, admires, and reveres,—of whatever most divinely expresses the essential meaning of the Christian faith and life; and to be torn away from the great company I have named, and transferred to the ranks which command a far fainter allegiance, is an unnatural, and for me an inadmissible fate." *

The way to test how the world would get on without Christianity is to examine how it *did* get on without it when the experiment was made under the most favourable circumstances. I have already said enough on that point, and I will not repeat it here. But for any one

* 'Strictures,' p. 5.

who has been born and bred in a Christian land to rail against Christianity and to advocate an undogmatic morality is, what yourself lately described it, "a terrible imposture." For my own part, I do not scruple to say that, of the two, I would rather see a people in possession of a true faith and given over to immorality, than in possession of a false faith or no faith at all, and living morally. And for this reason, that so long as a nation retains the true faith it possesses the means and the guarantee of a future regeneration. But let it give up its faith, and its morality will speedily follow, leaving no means of restoration behind.

But we are told that "words proper for one age may be quite unsuitable to another; and so this Creed, which was doubtless useful and proper when it was devised, seems quite inapplicable to our times, and why should we have it riveted for ever to the neck of the Church?"* I must say that I, for one, do not feel at all confident that the language of the Athanasian Creed is unsuitable to our time. On the contrary, I believe that its public recitation helps to keep down **more** than one latent heresy which would otherwise shoot above the ground and disseminate its noxious seed. It is impossible to read much of even the professedly religious literature of the day without finding traces of Arianism, Nestorianism, and Eutychianism;

---

* See Archdeacon Fearon's speech in Convocation, 'Guardian,' May 8.

and I decline altogether to admit, therefore, that the Athanasian Creed has become obsolete, and may be safely cast aside as an interesting, but useless relic from a bygone age.

But if the **case were** otherwise, and I felt quite sure that there was not even the germ of an ancient heresy in our **moral** and intellectual atmosphere; even then I should strongly deprecate the disuse of the Athanasian Creed. This is not a time in which old landmarks can be safely removed. On the contrary, there are many reasons which should induce us to do all we can to "strengthen the things that remain." Remember that if the Athanasian Creed is mutilated, or abolished, or its use made optional, it loses all its dogmatic authority, and no one can ever again appeal to it as a decisive touchstone of doctrine. Its authority, once gone, can never be restored. This point has **been** treated in so masterly a manner by Mr. Stuart **Mill,** that I shall make no apology for quoting the following somewhat long passage :

"In attempting to rectify **the use of** a vague term by giving it a fixed connotation, we must take care not to discard (unless advisedly, and on the ground of a deeper knowledge of the subject) any portion **of the** connotation which the word, in however indistinct a manner, previously carried with it. For otherwise language loses one of its inherent and **most valuable** properties, that of being the conservator of ancient experience; the keeper-alive of those thoughts and observations of former ages, which may be alien to the tendencies of the passing time. This function of language is so often overlooked or undervalued, that a few observations on it appear to be extremely required.

"Even when the connotation of a term has been accurately fixed, and still more if it has been left in the state of a vague unanalyzed feeling of resemblance; there is a constant tendency in the world, through familiar use, to part with a portion of its connotation. It is a well-known law of the mind that a word originally associated with a very complex cluster of ideas is far from calling up all those ideas in the mind every time the word is used; it calls up only one or two, from which the mind runs on by fresh associations to another set of ideas, without waiting for the suggestion of the remainder of the complex cluster. If this were not the case, processes of thought could not take place with anything like the rapidity which we know they possess. Very often, indeed, when we are employing a word in our mental operations, we are so far from waiting until the complex idea which corresponds to the meaning of the word is consciously brought before us in all its parts, that we run on to new trains of ideas by the other associations which the mere word excites, without having realized in our imagination any part whatever of the meaning: thus using the word, and using it well and accurately, and carrying on important processes of reasoning by means of it, in an almost mechanical manner, so much so, that some metaphysicians, generalizing from an extreme case, have fancied that all reasoning is but the mechanical use of a set of terms, according to a certain form. We may discuss and settle the most important interests of towns or nations by the application of general theorems or practical maxims previously laid down, without having had consciously suggested to us once in the whole process the houses and green fields, the thronged market-places and domestic hearths, of which not only those towns and nations consist, but which the word town and nation confessedly mean.

"Since, then, general names come in this manner to be used (and even to do a portion of their work well), without suggesting to the mind the whole of their meaning, and often with the suggestion of a very small, or no part at all, of that meaning; we cannot wonder that words so used come in time to be no longer capable of suggesting any other of the ideas appropriated to them than those with which the association is most immediate and strongest, or most kept up by the incidents of life: the remainder being lost altogether; *unless the mind, by often consciously dwelling on them, keeps up the association.* Words naturally retain much more of their meaning to persons of active imagination, who habitually represent to themselves things in the concrete, with the details which belong to them in the actual world. To minds of a different description the only antidote to this corruption of language is predication. The habit of predicating of the name all the various properties which it originally connoted keeps up the association between the name and those properties.

"But in order that it may do so, it is necessary that the predicates should themselves retain their association with the properties which they severally connote. For the proposition cannot keep the meaning of the words alive if the meaning of the propositions themselves should die. And nothing is more common than for propositions to be mechanically repeated, mechanically retained in the memory, and their truth undoubtingly assented to and relied on, while yet they carry no meaning distinctly home to the mind; and while the matter of fact or law of nature, which they originally expressed, is as much lost sight of, and practically disregarded, as if it never had been heard of at all. In those subjects which are at the same time familiar and complicated, and especially in those which are so in as great a degree as moral and social subjects are, it is matter of common remark how many important propositions are believed and repeated from habit, while no account could be given, and no sense is practically manifested, of the truths which they convey. Hence it is that the traditional maxims of old experience, though seldom questioned, have often so little effect on the conduct of life; because their meaning is never, by most persons, really felt until personal experience has brought it home. And thus also it is that so many doctrines of religion, ethics, and even politics, have manifested, after the association of that meaning with the verbal formulas has ceased to be kept up by the controversies which accompanied their first introduction, a tendency to degenerate rapidly into lifeless dogmas; which tendency **all** the efforts of an education expressly and skilfully directed to keeping the meaning alive are barely found sufficient to counteract.

"Considering, then, that the human mind, in different generations, occupies itself with different things and in one age is led by the circumstances which surround it to fix more of its attention upon one of the properties of a thing, in another age upon another; **it** is natural and inevitable that in every age a certain portion of our recorded experience and traditional knowledge, not being continually suggested by **the** pursuits and inquiries with which mankind are at that time engrossed, should fall asleep, as it were, and fade from the memory. *It would be in danger of being totally lost if the propositions or formulas, the results of the previous experience, did not remain, as forms of words it may be, but of words that once really conveyed, and are still supposed to convey, a meaning; which meaning, though suspended, may be historically traced, and, when suggested, may be recognized by minds of the necessary endowments as being still matter of fact, or truth. While the formulas remain the meaning may at any time revive;*

and as on the one hand the formulas progressively lose the meaning they were intended to convey; so on the other, when this forgetfulness has reached its height and begins to produce obvious consequences, minds arise which from the contemplation of the formulas rediscover the truth, when truth it was, which was contained in them, and announce it again to mankind, not as a discovery, **but as** *the meaning of that which they have been taught, and still profess to believe.*

"Thus there is a perpetual oscillation in spiritual (I do not mean religious) truths, and in spiritual doctrines of any significance, even when not truths. Their meaning is almost always in a process of being **lost or** of being recovered. Whoever has attended to the history of the more serious convictions of mankind—of the opinions by which the general conduct of their lives is, or as they conceive ought to be, more especially regulated—is aware that even when recognizing verbally the same doctrines, they attach to them at different periods a greater or a less quantity, and even a different kind, of meaning. The words in their original acceptation consisted, and the propositions expressed, a complication of outward facts and inward feelings, **to** different portions of which the general mind is more particularly alive in different generations of mankind. To common minds, only that portion of the meaning is in each generation suggested of which that generation possesses the counterpart in its own habitual experience. *But the words and propositions lie ready to suggest to any mind duly prepared the remainder of the meaning. Such individual minds are almost always to be found: and the lost meaning, revived by them, again by degrees works its way into the general mind.*

"The arrival of this salutary reaction may, however, be materially retarded *by the shallow conceptions and incautious proceedings of mere logicians.* It sometimes **happens** that towards the close of the downward period, when the words have lost part of their significance and have not yet begun to recover it, persons arise whose leading and favourite idea is the importance of clear conceptions and precise thought, and the necessity therefore of definite language. These persons, **in** examining the old formulas, easily perceive that words are used in them without a meaning ; *and if they are not the sort of persons who are capable of rediscovering the lost signification, they naturally enough dismiss* **the formula,** *and define the name without reference to it.* **In so** *doing they fasten down the name to what it connotes* **in** *common use at the time when it conveys the smallest quantity of meaning; and introduce the practice of employing it, consistently and uniformly, according to that connotation.* The word in this way acquires an extent of denotation far beyond what it had before; it becomes extended to many things to which it was previously, in appearance capriciously, refused. Of the propositions in which it was formerly used, those which are true in virtue of the forgotten part of its meaning **are** now, by **the** clearer light which the definition diffuses, seen not to be true according to the definition; which, however, is the recognized and sufficiently correct expression of all that **is** perceived **to be** in the mind of any one by **whom** the term is **used** at the present day. *The ancient formulas are consequently treated as prejudices; and people are no longer taught, as before, though not to understand them, yet to believe **that there is** truth in them. **They** no longer remain in the general mind surrounded by respect, and ready at any time to suggest their original meaning.* When they contain *truths, those truths are not only, in these circumstances, rediscovered far more slowly, **but** when re-discovered, the prejudice with which novelties **are** regarded is **now, in** some degree at least, against them, instead of being on their **side**.* . . . . . Language is the depository of the accumulated body of experience to which all former ages have contributed their part, and which is the inheritance **of** all yet to come. **We have** *no right **to** prevent ourselves from transmitting to posterity **a** larger portion of this inheritance than we may ourselves* **have** profited by. **We** can often improve greatly **on** the conclusions of our forefathers; but we ought **to** be careful not inadvertently to let any of their premisses slip through our fingers."*

* 'System of Logic,' ii., pp. 219-225. Cf. Hooker, b. v., ch. xiii., 13. "If time have worn **out, or any other** mean altogether taken **away** what was first intended, uses not thought upon before may

I will not weaken the argumentative force of this striking passage by any words of my own. Its applicability to the Athanasian Creed is obvious. At present that Creed is accepted as an authoritative exposition of doctrine throughout the whole Church. "It is the authoritative word of the Church," says Dr. Newman, "and the infallible answer of the Church to all her children who ask questions on the subject of which it speaks." "The Church," says the Senior Professor of Theology in Maynooth College, "is fully committed to the perfect purity of each doctrinal statement in the Athanasian Creed, just as much as if that purity had been defined by a General Council." And Dr. Döllinger, in a letter which he has kindly written to me on the subject, says that Roman Catholic theologians, "in their scholastic treatises on the Trinity and Incarnation, use the formulas contained in the Creed as a paramount authority." Hence, though the Creed has fallen out of popular use in the Roman Communion, its dogmatic authority remains unimpaired; it retains its place in an Office imposed on all the clergy, and meant theoretically for the laity also; none of its propositions have

afterwards spring up, and be reasonable causes of retaining that which other considerations did formerly procure to be instituted. And it cometh sometime to pass that a thing unnecessary in itself as touching the whole direct purpose whereto it was meant or can be applied, doth notwithstanding appear convenient to be still held even without use, lest by reason of that coherence which it hath with somewhat most necessary, the removal of the one should endamage the other."

been called in question, and no indignity has ever been put upon it. It is therefore still a living authoritative Creed, and consequently, as **Mr.** Mill says, "while the formulas remain, the meaning may at any time revive," however much it may be obscured or forgotten.

It is vain to pretend that this would be our case if any of the proposals for shelving the Athanasian Creed should receive the sanction of the Church of England. In the case of the Roman Catholic laity the Creed has simply undergone that process of obscuration so well described by Mr. Mill, and there are no "shallow conceptions and incautious proceedings of mere logicians" to impede a "salutary reaction." But if our "mere logicians" should unfortunately have their way, a stigma will be put upon the Creed; its meaning will be "fastened down to what it connotes in common use at the time when it conveys the smallest quantity of meaning"; and when a crisis arrives in which the Creed might be invaluable, "the ancient formulas are treated as prejudices; people are no longer taught, as before, though not to understand them, yet to believe that there is truth in them; they no longer remain in the general mind surrounded by respect, and ready at any time to suggest their original meaning." A Creed fallen into desuetude can always start into life when the appropriate occasion **arrives.** A Creed deposed deliberately and of set purpose becomes a corpse, and has no resurrection for those who have degraded it. In the one case there is suspended animation; in the other death.

I have not gone into the historical objections against the Athanasian Creed: partly because I am not scholar enough to examine the question thoroughly; but chiefly because, as I have already stated, I regard all such objections as absolutely irrelevant to the present controversy. Since, however, I have spoken somewhat disparagingly of Mr. Ffoulkes's Essay, I think I am bound in fairness to give some reasons for my opinion.

Mr. Ffoulkes's theory, then, stated briefly, is as follows. In about A.D. 800, Paulinus, Patriarch of Aquileia, compiled the so-called Athanasian Creed, and, with the help of Charlemagne and Alcuin, foisted it on a credulous world as a genuine composition of the great Athanasius. And this with the diabolical purpose of causing a schism between Eastern and Western Christianity!

This certainly is a sufficiently grave accusation against such hitherto irreproachable names as those of Alcuin and Paulinus, to say nothing of Charlemagne. There is a charitable old proverb which recommends us to say "nothing but good of the dead." But there are those who seem to think that when the grave has closed over a man, and he is no longer able to defend himself, his fair fame is a legitimate *corpus vile* on which any wanton libeller who has a crotchet to air is at liberty to try his experiments. "What excuse," asks Mr. Ffoulkes, "can be made for men devoted to God, like Alcuin, like Paulinus, who could assist in propagating what they **must have** known to be a fraud and a **lie?**" And what excuse, let me add, can be made for a man devoted to God, like Mr. Ffoulkes, who could make such an atrocious accusation against two great names on any evidence short of the clearest demonstrative proof? What proof, then, does Mr. Ffoulkes produce in support of his very serious accusation? None; absolutely none. Conjectures he gives us in abundance, but not a scrap of evidence that can stand a moment's cross-examination. But you shall judge for yourself. Mr. Ffoulkes's solitary proof that the Athanasian Creed was wickedly forged by Paulinus in the year 800 is an extract from a letter addressed to him in that year by Alcuin. Here is the precious extract, which I quote with Mr. Ffoulkes's italics, but without the **large type in** which he has arrayed a portion of it:—

"To my most beloved lord in the Lord of lords, and holy father, Patriarch Paulinus, greeting:

"I seem **to** have been refreshed inwardly, that the **hidden** flame of charity within my heart may be able to elicit **at** least some spark, lest that be extinguished which burns within me, now that I have opportunity to write something to one so dear. What! when I have the privilege of looking upon letters from you sweeter than honey, do I not seem to hold converse wholly with all the flowers of Paradise, and with the eager hand of desire to pluck from thence spiritual fruits? how much more, then, on perusing *the tract* ('libellum') *of your most holy faith,* adorned with all the *spotlessness of Catholic peace; eloquent and attractive in style to the highest degree; in the truth of its ideas firm as a rock* .... where, as from one bright and salutary fountain in Paradise, I beheld the streams of the four virtues irrigating not merely the rich plains of Italy, but *the entire demesne of ecclesiastical Latinity.* Where, too, *I beheld the golden outpourings of spiritual ideas commingling abundantly with the gems of scholastic polish.* Certainly you have achieved a work of immense profit and prime necessity *in appraising the Catholic faith as you have:* the very thing I have so long desired myself, and so often urged upon the King, to get a symbol of the Catholic faith, plain in meaning and lucid in phrase, reduced to **one** compendious form,' and given **to all priests in each** parish of every diocese to read, and commit to memory, so that everywhere the same faith might be uttered by **a** multitude of tongues. Lo! what I had desired in my humility, has been supplied by your genius. With the Author of our salvation you have earned for yourself a perpetual reward of this good intention, and *praise amongst men for this perfect work.*"

" I have printed in italics," says Mr. Ffoulkes, **"those** parts of it which I consider highly specific, and in large type what I consider absolutely distinctive. Most people will agree with me that one set of expressions is singularly descriptive of the Athanasian Creed: I hope to prove to their satisfaction that the other can describe nothing else."

I should be very sorry to say anything offensive of Mr. Ffoulkes; but if I am to speak my mind frankly I must say that this opinion of his seems to me to prove him to be absolutely destitute of the critical faculty. Let us look at those parts of Alcuin's letter which Mr. Ffoulkes considers "singularly descriptive" and "absolutely distinctive" of the Athanasian Creed. The "Libellus" which Alcuin praises, and which Mr. Ffoulkes seeks to identify with the Athanasian Creed, is described as "eloquent and attractive in style to the highest degree," and consisting of "the golden outpourings of spiritual ideas commingling abundantly with the gems of scholastic polish." A writer who thinks this description "singularly descriptive of the Athanasian Creed" appears to me to be "a reasoner not to be reasoned against," but in a sense very different from that in which Dr. Johnson applied that phrase to Leslie. "Eloquent and attractive in style to the highest degree" is surely the very last criticism that any person not in blind slavery to a crotchet would dream of making on the Athanasian Creed. That it abounds with "gems" I have no doubt at all; but they are certainly not "the gems of scholastic polish." Alcuin, moreover, calls the 'Libellus' of Paulinus "plain in meaning and lucid in phrase;" and it is this description which Mr. Ffoulkes "considers absolutely distinctive" of the Athanasian Creed. Well, there is no accounting for taste; but **Mr.** Ffoulkes's notions of what constitutes plainness of meaning and lucidity of phrase is certainly very different from that of the assailants of the Athanasian Creed. They have vexed the air with their complaints against what they consider its hard terminology and scholastic subtleties; and to be told that "plainness in meaning and lucidity in phrase" are characteristics of it which are "absolutely distinctive" must be to them a very funny suggestion. In fact, Mr. Ffoulkes appears to me to be quite incapable of appreciating the value of his own quotations. He undertakes to " prove to the satisfaction" of his readers that Alcuin's praise of Paulinus's 'Libellus' for being "plain in meaning and lucid in phrase" "can describe nothing else" but the Athanasian Creed. And how does he prove it? By quoting, five pages farther on, an injunction of Archbishop Hincmar to his clergy, ordering them to "commit to memory the discourse of Athanasius on the Faith, beginning with 'Whosoever will be saved;' so as to understand it thoroughly, *and be able to put it into plain language.*" Here we have the Archbishop of Rheims not only quoting the Athanasian Creed as "the discourse of Athanasius" within a few years of its alleged concoction by Paulinus, but actually instructing his clergy to study it carefully in order that they may "be able to put it into plain language;" it being already, according to Mr. Ffoulkes, so "plain in meaning and lucid in phrase" that such a description "can describe nothing else" but the Athanasian Creed! Is Mr. Ffoulkes really serious? Or is his book merely intended as an experiment on the credulity of the British public? He is a learned man, I know. But learning is the bane of a writer who has fallen under the slavery of a dominant crotchet. The French Jesuit, Jean Hardouin, was a learned man; yet he wrote an elaborate essay to prove that the Classics were written by monks in the Middle Ages, and urged in defence of his paradox the extraordinary plea that "it was no use getting up to read at four o'clock in the morning if, at the age of fifty, he was to think like other men!" I know not if Mr. Ffoulkes has reached the age of fifty; but he certainly seems ambitious to earn the reputation of not thinking like other men. No one, surely, who was not committed *per fas et nefas* to the establishment of a foregone conclusion, would venture on the following assertion:—"Its (Athanasian Creed's) age and authorship have been established from hence.—A.D. 800 Alcuin compliments Paulinus in a glowing letter addressed to him on having supplied a great need by a recent work of his, which is thereupon described in terms hardly capable of being improved upon had he been describing this (Athanasian) Creed."* I have quoted this "glowing letter," and I

* Mr. Ffoulkes 'On the Athanasian Creed,' p. 273.

appeal to you whether it would not be **more true to** say that whatever the document may be to which it refers, it is simply impossible that it can be the Athanasian Creed. The very points on which Mr. Ffoulkes relies disprove absolutely the conclusion which he seeks to extract from them; and, in addition, it is evident from Alcuin's letter that the 'Libellus' on which he is commenting contained an exposition of "the four virtues," not a trace of which is discoverable in the Athanasian Creed. Yet Mr. Ffoulkes assures us, with wearisome iteration, that in this very letter Alcuin **"has** solved a long-vexed historical problem for us of high interest, which, but for this stray letter of his, might never have been unlocked to the end of time, but which, touched with the key supplied here, tells its own tale, from beginning to end, in the simplest form." All this, and much like it, is said with such calm complacency that it **is** impossible to suspect the writer of an elaborate attempt **to gull** his readers. He really is not joking. He means what he says, and it is evident that he is not haunted by the slightest misgiving as to the perfect soundness of his reasoning. **Am** I not justified in saying that however learned such a writer may be, he is simply destitute of the critical faculty? If Mr. Ffoulkes's book is to pass as a specimen of good reasoning, all I can say is that, for the future, anything may be proved by anything.

"But if the Athanasian Creed was really the work of

Paulinus, how," Mr. Ffoulkes pertinently asks, "came the title which **it has** always borne to have been given to it?" How indeed? But Mr. Ffoulkes is equal to the occasion. "If people were christened after their patron saints, why should not their works be?" Is it really necessary to point out to Mr. Ffoulkes that **in** the one case there is no possibility of deception, in the other there is? "Besides," Mr. Ffoulkes goes on, "'Call your picture a Raphael or a Rubens, whatever its intrinsic excellencies, **if** you wish it to attract general notice,' is what people say still." I do not know who the people are who say so, and I rejoice that I have not the honour of their acquaintance. "But thirdly," says Mr. Ffoulkes, "Paulinus was *not* the publisher of his own work. It was taken out of his hands by his imperial master, and appropriated to a public purpose." Where did Mr. Ffoulkes learn this interesting fact? Where he learnt most of the *data* on which his theory is based—in the secret depths of his inner consciousness. Not a single scrap of evidence does he even pretend to adduce in support of it. This, I humbly venture to think, is a little too cool. Mr. Ffoulkes left the Church of Rome because he would not accept the dogma of Papal Infallibility. He must excuse me for saying that I decline to accept the origin of the Athanasian Creed on no better evidence than *his* personal infallibility; which is positively the only evidence that **he** has yet given to the world.

But I have not yet exhausted his oracular revelations. Paulinus, forsooth! may have had a *nom de plume.* "Why should it not have been Athanasius?" Very good, Mr. Ffoulkes; produce your evidence from contemporary sources. "Unfortunately," replies Mr. Ffoulkes, "there is not a grain of evidence in their writings—at least, in those that have come down to us—that he was ever known to them by that name." But what then? Is Mr. Ffoulkes's theory to collapse for lack of evidence? To avoid so dire a calamity Mr. Ffoulkes will manufacture evidence; and so he calmly suggests, with all the hushed emphasis of italics, that Paulinus, after all, *must* have had a *nom de plume;* but "*this his assumed name was known only to the initiated, and kept a profound secret from all else.*" Yet, after all, "it matters little whether this was so, or whether the name of St. Athanasius was given to the Creed alone, *so long as* **there** *was concealment.* And concealment in one way or other, and for some deliberate purpose, there must have been, otherwise the origin of this Creed could not have remained so long a mystery."[*]

I really feel that I owe you an apology for giving you the trouble of reading such childish stuff as this. But since Mr. Ffoulkes's book has been puffed into a degree of notoriety which its merits would never have secured for it, I must ask leave to inflict upon you one or two more specimens of his method of reasoning.

[*] 'On the Athanasian Creed,' pp. 240-242.

His theory is that the Athanasian Creed was forged by Paulinus about the year 800, with the guilty connivance of Alcuin. And certainly if Alcuin connived at the fraud at all, it must be owned that he did it on the " Pecca fortiter" principle. For we find him, within a year or two of the alleged compilation of the Creed by Paulinus, writing of it thus :—

" The blessed Athanasius, the most revered Bishop of the city of Alexandria, then . . . in the 'Exposition of the Catholic faith,' *which the illustrious doctor himself composed*, and which the Universal Church professes, declares the procession of the Holy Spirit from the Father and the Son in these words."

And then follows a quotation from the Athanasian Creed as we have it now. We are asked to believe therefore, without a grain of evidence, that our own great Alcuin was such an unprincipled scamp as to declare deliberately, in a set treatise, that the Athanasian Creed was really composed by Athanasius himself, having just about the same time, and in a letter apparently **not** meant to be confidential, ascribed it to Paulinus. We are to believe, further, that this fraud was perpetrated for the fell purpose of destroying the Unity of the Catholic Church. And, last of all, we are to believe that, in addition to being an astute rogue, Alcuin was, withal, such an egregious fool as to declare publicly of a forged Creed, of which the ink was scarcely dry, that " the Universal Church professed it."

With one more specimen of Mr. Ffoulkes's "short method" of reaching his conclusions, I shall take leave of the most abortive essay in historical criticism that it has ever been my lot to peruse. In the year 798 Bishop Denebert, on his consecration to the See of Worcester, made a confession of faith in which occurs this passage:—

"Ego autem juxta ritum sacri nostri canonis et secundum ecclesiasticam regulam quemadmodum virium possibilitas permittit, omnem obedientiæ famulatum cum intima cordis devotione, una cum omnibus qui mecum sunt in Domino, tuis piis præceptis exhibiturum esse, veridico fine tenus profiteor ore; insuper et orthodoxam catholicam apostolicamque fidem sicut didici, paucis exponam verbis, *quia scriptum est*, 'Quicunque vult salvus esse ante omnia opus est illi ut teneat catholicam fidem.'" *

And then the Bishop proceeds to quote a portion of the Athanasian Creed. Now let it be remembered that according to Mr. Ffoulkes's hypothesis the Athanasian Creed was composed in or about A.D. 800. Probably 800; for Alcuin's letter, written in that year, implies that the 'Libellus' which he criticizes had just been published. Yet here we have an English Bishop quoting the Athanasian Creed in the year 798, and quoting it in such a way as to imply that it was then a well-known confession of faith.

* 'Councils and Ecclesiastical Documents,' by Stubbs and Haddan, p. 526.

It was, of course, impossible for Mr. Ffoulkes to ignore Denebert's profession of faith, for Waterland makes a point of it. But he gets over the difficulty, *more suo*, by a series of conjectures which have absolutely not the shadow of a foundation in fact. He will not believe **that Denebert** could have learnt a confession of faith, embodying a **portion of** the Athanasian Creed, from anybody but Alcuin. " Who had put it into his mouth? Why not Alcuin? Alcuin had **many** disciples in England, of whom Denebert *may have been* one; was always corresponding with them; *and would be sure to give them the earliest intelligence of a new work by Paulinus.* When he wrote to express his admiration of it to its author, it had not been named—*perhaps* contained no damnatory clauses **at all,** but the first. And Alcuin *may have simultaneously quoted the first half of it* as a specimen to Denebert, whose consecration was impending; for the dates in each case are **too** close, without either being fixable to a year, to present any difficulty. . . . Alcuin's letter, for instance, *may have been* written a year sooner; *or Denebert's consecration a year later.*"*

And it is on the strength of absurd criticism like this that **we are** seriously called upon to give up the Athanasian **Creed!** Read again Alcuin's letter, on which the whole **of** Mr. Ffoulkes's theory hangs, and you can hardly doubt **that the** 'Libellus,' which he praises so highly, had just appeared. **Now** Alcuin's letter was

* 'On the Athanasian Creed,' p. 296.

written in the year 800. And yet two years before this date an English Bishop quotes the Athanasian Creed as a document then well known in England. *Quia Scriptum est* is not the way in which a newly published tract would have been quoted. The phrase implies at once the antiquity and the public authority of the document. And we are to set aside this conclusive evidence because an impracticable crotchet-monger in the nineteenth century thinks fit to suggest that the facts " may have been," " **perhaps** " were, " would be sure " to be otherwise! Mr. Ffoulkes believes that the Athanasian Creed was concocted, for the worst of purposes, by a triumvirate of fraudulent liars, namely, Charlemagne, Paulinus, and Alcuin; and if the facts do not square with his theory, so much the worse for the facts. *Ffoulkes locutus est, causa finita est.* Witness the following suggestion :—" If we should say that the damnatory clauses of the Athanasian Creed were dictated by him (Charlemagne) originally, or inserted with his own hand in revising it, we should probably not be far wrong."* Why? Simply because Mr. Ffoulkes chooses to say so. We are to accept the *dicta* of his infallible imagination, not merely in lieu of facts, but in spite of them. There is not one of his conclusions which is not based on an " if," a " perhaps," a " may have been " or a " probably;" and he does not seem to take it to heart that his various hypotheses do not

* 'On the Athanasian Creed,' p. 260.

hang together, but that, on the contrary, like the pots which went sailing down the stream, they crack each other. And yet he has the assurance to wind up his argument, if a conclusion without premisses may be called an argument, in the following manner:

"This, then, is the solution of the mystery that has so long enveloped the Athanasian Creed. It was at once the expression of Latin dogmatism and the lever of Latin despotism: a symbol of the impending subjugation of the Church of Christ, both in thought and act, to a spirit which was neither of Jerusalem, nor yet of Grece, but of Rome—of Rome first pagan, and then Christian. Every time we recite the Athanasian Creed it is reason not Scripture that speaks:* Charlemagne not Athanasius that expounds: a faith deliberately set up in opposition to the faith of Nicæa and Constantinople that is professed. All this is incontrovertible, unless the facts which have been adduced are not facts." †

"Unless the facts which have been adduced are not facts!" Why, he has not adduced a single fact which does not tell against his theory. And as to the Athanasian Creed being "a faith deliberately set up in opposition to the faith of Nicæa and Constantinople," I will only say that the man who could make such an assertion proves himself to be as deficient in theo-

---

* Does Mr. Ffoulkes mean to imply that reason and Scripture are in opposition to each other? His words can have no other meaning.

† 'On the Athanasian Creed,' p. 276.

logical, as he has abundantly proved himself to be in critical, acumen.

And now I take my leave of Mr. Ffoulkes. I should be sorry to hurt his feelings unnecessarily; but I must say plainly that a man who deliberately sets himself to disturb the faith of Christendom and to traduce, without a scintilla of evidence, the characters of great men who were benefactors of their race, and who lived and died without reproach, deserves no consideration. Mr. Ffoulkes would not dare to publish such a libel on the characters of living men. Does he think that he owes no duty of charity or justice to the dead?

It will be a relief to you, I have no doubt, to be assured that I am drawing to the close of this long letter—the longest, probably, that any correspondent has ever inflicted on you. The subject is a very fruitful one, and my pen has already run on to a length far beyond my intention when I began to write. There are still a number of points on which I have not touched, and on which I should like very much to enlarge; but I am afraid of wearying you, and I shall therefore compress what I have still to say into very narrow compass.

One of the objections to the Athanasian Creed is that it rests man's salvation on a speculative belief in a **number of** theological propositions, to the disparagement of practical morality. No charge could be more **untrue.** The conclusion of **the whole Creed is** that holiness of life and orthodoxy of faith are inseparably connected. "They that *have done good* shall go into life everlasting, and they that *have done evil* into everlasting fire. This is the Catholic Faith, which except a man believes faithfully he cannot be saved." Everlasting salvation is made to hinge, therefore, not on the barren assent of the intellect to certain dogmatic propositions, but on a faith eventuating in good works. Even men of latitudinarian opinions in matters of religion have been fain to admit this. The late Dr. Donaldson, for instance, speaks of the Athanasian Creed as "a symbol or Creed not less distinguished from other documents of the same class by the logical accuracy of its theological statements than by the earnestness with which it insists on the necessity of a sober, righteous, and godly life."*

Another accusation against the Athanasian Creed is that it narrows the basis of Church Communion by practically excommunicating all who do not accept its technical phraseology. Instead of answering this objection myself, I shall take the liberty of quoting at length the answer of one who incurred no small unpopularity in his lifetime for propounding what many thought lax and dangerous views on some of the religious questions of the day. I mean Dr. Donaldson, to whom I have already referred. The following passage occurs in his 'Christian Orthodoxy' (pp. 467–470):—

"It is a mistake to suppose that a Creed, at the time

* 'Christian Orthodoxy,' p. 465.

when it is put forth, is intended to narrow the basis of the Church. The obvious purpose of such a Symbol or passport of admission into a Church must be to include as many as possible, and this not so much by precise and logical statements of what the believer must profess, as by negativing certain propositions which tended to break up the Church into a number of sects. As we have shown in the text, the Church Catholic, and even a national Church, is necessarily more comprehensive than any community of men who dissent on particular grounds. It has been well remarked, that even the othodox settlements of the Creed 'were in fact expressions of dogma, which did act as comprehensions in their time. As, for instance, even the final expression of the doctrine of the consubstantiality of the Son with the Father comprehended as many as could possibly be comprehended within the terms of one and the same profession, considering the antagonistic theories between which that declaration placed itself;' so that 'the heterodox parties commenced the war of limitations,' and 'sought by definitions to narrow the Church of Christ,' whereas the orthodox party merely swept away these specialities.—(Wilson, 'Bampton Lectures,' p. 55.)

"In asserting the doctrine of the Trinity, the Athanasian Creed is much more engaged in contradicting erroneous views than in binding down the professors of Christianity to any particular theory on the subject. In asserting generally both an Unity of Godhead and a Trinity of Persons, this Creed meets with a contradiction all the mischievous theories which had originated from that doctrine. The heresies specially combated are the Arian, Sabellian, Nestorian, Eutychian, and Apollinarian. We have seen that false religion generally assumes one of three forms—*polytheism, dualism,* or *pantheism.* The *polytheistic* view of the doctrine of the Trinity would convert the three persons into three Gods, or establish a tritheism instead of an unity of Godhead. To this the Athanasian Creed opposes itself by a series of repeated contradictions from the seventh verse to the nineteenth, both inclusive. In passing from the crudest form of false religion to the antagonistic monotheism, the advocate of the orthodox faith in the Trinity had to combat two erroneous applications of that true belief. Monotheism sometimes represented itself as a recognition of one Supreme Deity, with certain ministerial agents subordinated to him, who constituted a class of secondary gods. This view was applied to the Trinity by Arius, who was thus guilty of a division of the divine Substance or entity. On the other hand, monotheism appeared as a recognition of only one God, who, however, acted upon or in the world by a merely temporary personification of Himself. This was the view applied to the explanation of the Trinity by Sabellius, who thus fell into the error of confusing the Persons. It will be seen that the Arian theory verged towards polytheism and represented the views of the Greeks; καὶ γὰρ κἀκεῖνοι, says Athanasius (*c. Arian.* iii., 16, p. 423, Newman's translation), ὥσπερ καὶ οὗτος, τῇ κτίσει λατρεύουσι παρὰ τὸν κτίσαντα τὰ πάντα θεόν; and he adds that this is really a kind of polytheism: 'the Arians are greater traitors than the Jews in denying the Christ, and they wallow (συγκυλίονται) with the Gentiles, hateful as they are to God (θεοστυγεῖς), worshipping the creature and many deities.' On the other hand, Sabellianism inclined to the Judaism of the times before the Exile, when God appeared among men by his angles or *mal'hakim*, and so Basil said that Sabellianism was merely Judaism under the form of Christianity (*Ep.* 210, 3: Ἰουδαϊσμός ἐστιν ὁ Σαβελλισμὸς ἐν προσχήματι Χριστιανισμοῦ; cf. Euseb. *c. Marcellum*, i. 8). These two antagonistic theories are contradicted together in the *Symbolum Quicunque*, vv. 3–6. As the *polytheistic* view was represented in greater or less degrees by Tritheism and Arianism, so the *dualistic* error found its approximation in the doctrines of Nestorius, who asserted that in Christ there were not only two natures but two persons; and *pantheism* asserted itself in the hypothesis of Eutyches, who denied the two natures in Christ, and maintained that the human was swallowed up in the divine. This latter doctrine, that of the Monophysites, as it is called, seems to have originated in the views of Apollinaris in the previous century, who held that Christ could not have had a human soul; that the *Word* dwelling in him must have been his only source of reasoning and information; and this was of course a denial of the two perfect natures, and an approximation to *pantheism*. Opposed as they were in other respects, it seems that the *pantheism* of Apollinaris inclined to the *polytheism* of Arius, and the *dualism* of Nestorius to the *monotheism* of Sabellius. 'If,' says Dr. Newman (*on Athanas.* ii. p. 292), 'the opposites of connected heresies are connected together, then the doctrinal connection of Arianism and Apollinarianism is shown in their respective opposition to the heresies of Sabellius and Nestorius. Salij (*Eutych. aut Eut.* 10) denies the connection, but with very little show of reason. La Croze calls Apollinarianism *Arianismi tradux* (*Thes. Ep. Lacroz.* t. 3, p. 276).' The Athanasian Creed stands in no direct antagonism to the Eutychians, whose views were not published till a later part of the same century, but their positions are fully denied by anticipation in vv. 27–35. Apollinaris, however, is referred to and contradicted in v. 30, where it is stated that 'Jesus Christ was perfect God and perfect man of a *reasonable soul* and human flesh subsisting;' and there is an equally immediate rebuke to Nestorius in v. 32, where it is added that although Jesus 'be God and man, yet He is *not two but one* Christ.'

"In thus putting a veto on the precise limitations of belief, which would have narrowed the Catholic Church to the dimensions of a dogmatic sect, **the** *Symbolum Quicunque* does not itself advance any theory **respecting** the **Trinity**. Its doctrine is given in

vv. 20-26, and these statements are followed by the assertion of a real incarnation, of the fact that Christ, whose divinity had been previously maintained, was in every sense a human being also—' God, of the substance of his Father, begotten before the world; and man, of the substance of his mother, born in the world'—and therefore 'equal to the Father, as touching his Godhead, and inferior to the Father, as touching his manhood.' The doctrine of the Trinity, thus generally conceived, is, as we have shown in the text, not speculative but practical, and capable of leading directly to holiness of heart and life."*

I think I have sufficiently exposed the fallacy of arguing for the abolition of the Athanasian Creed on the plea that it is not used in the congregational services of the Church of Rome. But there is one answer at which I have only hinted, and which I will now state somewhat more fully. It is true, as I have already admitted, that the office of Prime, in which the Athanasian Creed occurs, has almost entirely ceased to be a lay service in the Roman communion. But it is still in theory, as it originally was in practice, an office intended quite as much for the laity as for the clergy; and its restriction to clerical use is one of those abuses which the Reformers professed to abolish when they rearranged the Ancient Offices for the avowed purpose

* 'Christian Orthodoxy,' pp. 467-470.

of making them congregational. It is an abuse, too, which some of the most distinguished members of the Church of Rome lament, and of which they would be very glad to get rid. "There can be no doubt," says the late Cardinal Wiseman, "that, while the ancient Christians had their thoughts constantly turned towards God in private prayer, the Church took care to provide for all the regular and necessary discharge of this duty, *by her public offices.* These were not meant to be holiday services; *or mere clerical duties; but the ordinary daily, and sufficient discharge of an obligation belonging to every state and class in the Church.* . . . Unfortunately those offices have, for the most part, been **reduced to a** duty discharged by the clergy in private, and have thus come to be considered by us as a purely ecclesiastical obligation superadded, not comprehending, the discharge of ordinary Christian duty. *One is apt to forget that Prime is the Church's morning prayer, and Complin her evening devotion.* . . . Why should not this be restored? Why should they not become the standard devotions of all Catholics, whether alone or in their families? . . . We strongly suspect that many who will join the Church will hail with joy every such return, however imperfect, to the discipline and practice of the ancient Church; they will warm to us the more in proportion to our zeal for the restoration of its discipline."*

* 'Essays on Various Subjects,' by his Eminence Cardinal Wiseman, i., pp. 386, 395, 396.

In the Roman Church, therefore, the office of Prime, and with it the Athanasian Creed, may be restored to the use of the laity. But if the Church of England deliberately gives up the Athanasian Creed, its use can never again be restored, and English theology will receive a blow from which it may never recover. Look at what has been passing within the last few days on the other side of the English Channel. The Protestants of France, after an interval of two centuries, have met in synod and surveyed their theological position. And what is the result? They have gradually been drifting into open infidelity; so that, in the language of the intelligent and well-informed Paris correspondent of the 'Guardian,' "the Established French Protestant Church sank to little more than half a million of members who could in any real sense of the term be called Christians out of the forty millions of the French population by whom they are surrounded. And there they have remained ever since, without any defined rule of faith whatever, and having only succeeded by very small majorities in some of their Consistories—as here in Paris, for instance—in ejecting from their pulpits avowed infidels of the Renan School."*

Such is the consequence of keeping Creeds as "historical monuments." Two centuries ago the Athanasian Creed was a living expression of Faith both among the Calvinists of France and Switzerland and among the

* See 'Guardian,' June 19, 1872.

Lutherans of Germany. But its use, from being obligatory, became optional, and that soon degenerated into general disuse. We have seen the result to which this has led in France. In Switzerland the collapse of the Christian Faith has long been apparent; and the Prussian correspondent of 'The Times' has lately painted in melancholy colours the state of "Religious Thought in Germany."

"Who that knows modern Germany will call it a Christian land, either in the sense Rome gives to the term or in the meaning Luther attaches to it? . . . The Augsburg Confession, to maintain which Germany in the Thirty Years' **War** suffered herself to be cut to pieces by Austria and Austria's allies, has long ceased to be the authority it was; and, instead of the adamantine foundation of public belief, is now-a-days a mere ornamental decoration appended to the intellectual *status* of the land. In whatever section of society you may happen to move, there is the undeniable fact that the dogmatism of **St. Athanasius** and the statutes of the Council of Nice* have entirely ceased to be a living power. Scholars have begun to denominate Christianity an Asiatic religion; **and the** public, **proud of** their vaunted European enlightenment, accept the degrading name. . . . The truth is, that the majority of the educated, in their insidious march towards Rationalism, have advanced beyond acknowledging the necessity of **any Creed**. Not content

* The author means the Athanasian and Nicene Creeds.

with rejecting the Bible, whose dogmas they regard as entirely exploded by the moral, historical, and scientific criticism of the day, they have begun to doubt whether any teaching on transcendental subjects can be required to promote virtue. . . . There is a strong and growing impression that the Christian Creed has become too obsolete for anyone to take the trouble of warring against it."*

Let the Church of England upset the present *status* of the Athanasian Creed—a *status* which we have inherited uninterruptedly from the Reformation—and she will take the first downward step on the declivity which leads to infidelity. Not till the Creed has been abolished shall we know what we owe to it, not only as individuals, but as a nation. The public recitation of it helps almost more than anything else, I believe, to resist that continual tendency to shed portions of its intrinsic meaning, on which Mr. Mill, in a passage already quoted, has animadverted as common to all ancient formulas. Many a man, who declaims fiercely against it, owes to the swing of its rhythmical clauses his impression of the cardinal facts of Christianity, and especially his vivid image of that unique character in history, Jesus of Nazareth, the Eternal Son of God.† And as for those who believe that this is one of those questions which test to the quick the vitality of a

---

* 'Religious Thought in Germany.' By 'The Times' Correspondent at Berlin, pp. 26–28.   † See Appendix, Note D.

P

Church, there is no sacrifice which they will think too great to make in defence of what is to them dearer than anything this world can offer in exchange. I, for one, will never consent to recite the Athanasian Creed as a matter of individual option; and if the Church of England should commit herself to a policy so cowardly and so fatal, I should feel that I had no choice but to retire from her service. I know well, no one knows better, that this resolution of mine would matter to nobody in the world except myself. But there are others of whom this cannot be said. The Church of England cannot afford a secession from the Ministry led by such men as Dr. Pusey and Dr. Liddon. And it is probable that relinquishment of ministerial duties would not be confined to the school represented by those names. The Bishop of Lincoln has uttered some ominous hints; and even so moderate a man as Dean Goulburn has declared publicly that any interference with the Creed " would lead him seriously to reconsider his own position as an ordained minister of the Church."* So that the assailants of the Creed may find, when too late, that they have " made a solitude and called it peace."

But I have better hope of the future of the Church of England, and of the wisdom of her rulers; and I cannot conclude this letter more appropriately than by calling attention to the remarkable words of Count

* 'Reasons for neither Mutilating nor Muffling the Athanasian Creed.' By Edward Goulburn, D.D., Dean of Norwich, p. 37.

de Maistre, with your own published comment upon them twenty-two years ago:—

"Si jamais les Chrétiens se rapprochent, comme tout les y invite, il semble que la motion doit partir de l'Église d'Angleterre. Le Presbytérianisme fut une œuvre Française, et par conséquent une œuvre exagérée. Nous sommes trop éloignés des sectateurs d'un culte trop peu substantiel : il n'y a pas moyen de nous entendre, mais l'Église Anglicane, qui nous touche d'une main, touche de l'autre ceux que nous ne pouvons toucher ; et quoique, sous un certain point de vue, elle soit en butte aux coups des deux partis, et qu'elle présente le spectacle un peu ridicule d'un révolté qui prêche l'obéissance, cependant elle est très précieuse sous autres aspects, et peut-être, considérée comme un de ces intermédes chimiques, capables de rapprocher des élémens inassociables de leur nature."

On this striking testimony to the providential position of the English Church from the pen of a foreigner, and also an Ultramontane of the Ultramontanes, you comment as follows:—

"It is nearly sixty years since thus a stranger and an alien, a stickler to the extremest point for the prerogatives of his Church, and nursed in every prepossession against ours, nevertheless turning his eye across the Channel, though he could then only see her in the lethargy of her organization, and the dull twilight of her learning, could nevertheless discern that there was a special work written of God for her in heaven, and that she was VERY PRECIOUS to the Christian world. Oh! how serious a rebuke to those who, not strangers, but suckled at her breast, not two generations back, but the witnesses now of her true and deep repentance, and of her reviving zeal and love, yet (under whatever provocation) have written concerning her even as men might write that were hired to make a case against her, and by an adverse instinct in the selection of evidence, and a severity of construction, such as no history of the deeds of man can bear, have often in these last years put her to an open shame! But what a word of hope and encouragement to every one who, as convinced in his heart of the glory of her providential mission, shall unshrinkingly devote himself to defending within her borders the full and whole doctrine of the Cross, with that mystic symbol now as ever gleaming down on him from heaven, now as ever showing forth its inscription: *in hoc signo vinces.*"*

It is in the spirit of these eloquent words that I offer this humble contribution to the defence of the Athanasian Creed; and thanking you very sincerely for allowing me to address my remarks to you, I beg to subscribe myself, with feelings of unfeigned respect,

Yours very faithfully,

MALCOLM MACCOLL.

12, CHESTER TERRACE, EATON SQUARE,
    JUNE 15TH, 1872.

* 'Remarks on the Royal Supremacy,' pp. 87-88.

APPENDIX.

Note A (p. 25).

The following is the passage in Bishop Cotton's Charge referred to on p. 25 :—

"But, as in the case of the Baptismal Service, so in that of the Athanasian Creed, there is much to be learned from coming to India. One who resides in the midst of a heathen nation begins to realize the state of things in which the Apostles wrote those passages of which the Baptismal Service is a faithful echo, and in which the Primitive Bishops and Fathers of the Church drew up their confessions of faith. For the errors rebuked in the Athanasian Creed resulted from tendencies common to the human mind everywhere, and especially prevalent in this country. We cannot too strongly impress on those who recoil from its definitions and distinctions that its object was not to limit but to widen the pale of the Church, which various heretical sects were attempting to contract. It contains no theory of the Divine nature, but contradicts certain false opinions about it, and states the revealed truths of the Trinity and Incarnation without any attempt to explain them. It especially censures four errors: —The heresy of Arius, who 'divided the substance' of the Godhead by teaching that the Father was the supreme and the Son an inferior Deity; of Sabellius, who 'confounded the Persons' by supposing that the Father took our nature as the Man Christ Jesus, and after dying for our salvation operates on our hearts as the Holy Ghost; of Nestorius, who so completely separated our Lord's Divinity and humanity as to teach that he is not one but two Christs; and of Apollinaris, who asserted that He **was** not perfect **Man, with a** reasonable (or rational) soul, **but** a Being, in whom **the Godhead** supplied the place of the human intellect. Now these four tendencies **correspond to four forms** of error which are in full activity among us here. The chief cause of the horror with which Arianism was regarded by the Fathers of Nicæa was that it led directly back to the polytheism from which Constantine had **just** delivered the Roman Empire! Had it prevailed, Christianity would have been degraded into the worship of three Gods, the Father, the Son, and the Holy Ghost, with the Father as the Lord and Ruler of the other two. Arianism, therefore, so far as it was polytheistic, resembled the religion of the common people of this country. The theory of Sabellius, fatal to the truths of Christ's Mediation and Atonement, arose from that bare and unsympathizing monotheism which has since been erected by Mahomet into **a rival** and hindrance **to** the Gospel. The foremost of Indian sects in public spirit and intelligence inherit from their Persian ancestors the doctrine of two co-ordinate and independent principles, Ormuzd and Ahriman, Good and Evil, with the first of which Spirit, and with the other Matter, is immediately connected. From a tendency to this **very** same error, Nestorius separated altogether Christ's Divine from His human nature, although such a view **leads to** the denial that this world is redeemed from evil, and that man's body, **as** well as his soul and spirit, must be consecrated to God's service. The creed of many among the educated classes of India, and of not a few, I fear, in Europe, is the theory of pantheism, which quenches in us the love of God, since we cannot feel affection for One who has no personal attributes, and which is at least fatal to morality, by teaching that evil is only an inferior stage of good, 'good in the making,' as some one has expressed it, so that the two are in fact identical, each having alike its origin in God. From pantheistic sympathies Apollinaris, the precursor of Eutyches, was led to merge Christ's **Manhood** in His Godhead, and to deny that He had **a human** soul. Now if we remember that all these heresies sprang from tendencies which have given birth to separate religions of widely extended influence, in the midst of which we in India are living, we may surely pause before we expunge **from** the records of our Church an ancient protest against the application of these tendencies to Christianity, since, whenever the educated classes of this country embrace the Gospel, there will be need of watchfulness, lest its simplicity be perverted by the revival of errors which **all** had their origin in Eastern philosophy!"

Note B (see p. 143).

"We are by nature the Sons of Adam. When God **created** Adam He created us; and as many as are descended from Adam have in themselves the root out of which they spring. The sons of God we neither are all, nor any one of us, otherwise than only by grace and favour. The sons of God have God's own natural Son as a Second **Adam** from heaven, whose race and progeny they are by spiritual and heavenly birth. God therefore ~~being~~ [loving] eternally His Son, He must needs eternally in Him have loved and preferred **before** all others them which are spiritually sithence descended and sprung out of Him. . . . Our being in Christ by eternal foreknowledge saveth us not without our actual and real adoption into the fellowship of His Saints in this present world. For in Him we are, by actual incorporation into that Society which hath **Him** for their Head; and doth make together with Him one body (He and they in that respect having one name), for which cause, by virtue of this mystical conjunction, **we are** of Him, and in Him, even as though our very flesh and bones should be made continuate with His. . . . **The** Church is in Christ as Eve was in Adam. Yea, by **grace, we are** every of us in Christ, and **in** His Church, as by nature we were in those our first parents. God made Eve of the rib of Adam; and His Church He frameth out of the very flesh, the very wounded and bleeding side of the Son of Man. His Body crucified and His Blood shed for the life of the world are the True Elements of that heavenly Being which maketh us such as Himself is of whom we come. For which cause the words of Adam may be fitly **the words of** Christ concerning His Church, 'Flesh of **My** flesh, and bone of **My** bones;' a true native extract out of **My own Body.** So that in Him, even according **to** His Manhood, **we** according **to** our heavenly being are as branches in that root out of which they grow. To all things He is life, and to men light, as the Son of God; to the Church both life and light eternal by being made the Son of Man for us, and by being in us a Saviour, whether we respect Him as God or as Man. Adam is in us as an original cause of our nature, and of that corruption of nature which causeth death, Christ as the original cause of restoration to life. The person of Adam is not us, but his nature, and the corruption of his nature derived **into all** men by propagation; Christ having Adam's nature as **we** have, but incorrupt, deriveth not nature but incorruption, and that immediately from His own Person, with all that belong unto Him. As therefore we are really partakers of the body of sin and death, received from Adam, **so** except we be truly partakers of Christ, and as really possessed of His Spirit, all we speak of eternal life is but a dream. That which quickeneth us is the Spirit of the

Second Adam, *and His Flesh that wherewith He quickeneth*. That which in Him made our nature incorrupt was the union of His Deity with our nature. And in that respect the sentence of death and condemnation, which only taketh hold upon sinful flesh, could no way possibly extend unto Him. . . . These things St. Cyril duly considering reproveth their speeches which taught that only the Deity of Christ is the Vine whereupon we by Faith do depend **as** branches, and **that** neither His flesh nor our bodies are comprised in this resemblance. *For doth any man doubt but that even from the flesh of Christ our very bodies do receive that life which shall make them glorious at the latter day, and for which they are already accounted parts of His blessed Body?* Our contemptible bodies could never live the life they shall live, were it not that here they are joined with His Body, which is incorruptible, and that His is in ours as a cause of immortality, a cause by removing through the death and merit of His own flesh that which hindered the life of ours. Christ is therefore, *both as God and as man*, that true Vine whereof we both spiritually and corporally are branches. . . . It greatly offendeth that some, when they labour to show the use of the Holy Sacraments, assign unto them no end but only to *teach* the mind, by other senses, that which the Word doth teach by hearing. Whereupon how easily neglect and careless regard of so heavenly mysteries may follow we see in part **by** some experience had of those men with whom that opinion is most strong. For where the word of God may be heard, which teacheth with much more expedition anything we have to learn, if all the benefits we **reap by** Sacraments be instruction, they which at all times have opportunity of using the better means to that purpose, will surely hold the worse in less estimation. And unto infants which are not capable of instruction who would not think it a mere superfluity that any Sacrament is administered, if to administer the Sacraments be but to teach receivers what God doth for them? There is of Sacraments therefore undoubtedly some other more excellent and heavenly use. . . . That saving grace which Christ originally is or hath for the general good of His whole Church, by Sacraments He severally deriveth into every member thereof. Sacraments seem as the instruments of God to that end and purpose, moral instruments, the use whereof is in our hands, the effect in His. . . . We receive Christ Jesus in Baptism once as the first beginner, in the Eucharist often as being by continued degrees the finisher of our life. By Baptism therefore we receive Christ Jesus, and from Him that saving grace which is proper unto Baptism. By the other Sacrament we receive Him also, *imparting therein Himself*, and that grace which the Eucharist properly bestoweth. . . . The grace which we have by the Holy Eucharist doth not begin but continue life. No man therefore receiveth this Sacrament before Baptism, because no dead thing is capable of nourishment. That which groweth must of necessity first live. If our bodies did not daily waste, food to restore them were a thing superfluous. And it may be that the grace of Baptism would serve to eternal life were it not that the state of our spiritual being is daily **so much** hindered and impaired after Baptism. . . . Life being therefore proposed unto all men as their end, they which by Baptism have laid the foundation and attained the first beginning of a new life have here their nourishment and food presented for *continuance of life* in them. Such as will live the life of Christ must eat the Flesh and drink the Blood of the Son of Man, because this is a part of that diet which if we want we cannot live. . . . Our souls and bodies quickened to eternal life are effects the cause whereof is the Person of Christ; His Body and Blood are the true well-spring out of which this life floweth. So that His Body and Blood are in that very subject whereunto they minister life; not only by effect or operation, even as the influence of the heavens is in plants, beasts, men, and in everything which they quicken; but also by a far more Divine and mystical kind of union, which maketh us one with Him, even as He and the Father are one."—('Ecclesiastical Polity,' v. lvi., lvii., lxvii.)

It is true that Hooker goes on to say that "the Real Presence of Christ's Most Blessed Body and Blood is not therefore to be sought for in the Sacrament, but in the worthy receiver of the Sacrament." But he adds that "these Holy mysteries . . . impart to us, even in true and real, though mystical, manner, *the very Person of our Lord Himself, whole, perfect, and entire.*" This surely is inconsistent with anything short of an objective Presence—a Presence, that is, which is independent of man, and is imparted to him through the external agency of the Sacrament. Evidently what Hooker was anxious to guard against was the notion that the Sacrament could benefit men as a charm, without its hidden power coming in contact with their souls through participation. The Presence is there, in the Sacrament, but **only the** worthy communicant can really partake of it.

Note C (p. 160).

I was much gratified to find the view I have taken of the Sacramental principle confirmed after my remarks were in the press by one of those thoughtful articles which are such a marked feature of the 'Spectator.' Coming from so independent a source, the article is worth quoting; and here it is:—

. . . . "And whatever ought in point of fact to be surprising or otherwise, certainly no one can have the smallest acquaintance with the teaching of Christ and His Apostles without seeing that thoughts of this kind lay at the very basis of their doctrine, that in that teaching the material world is often treated as spiritual, and the spiritual world as material; that spiritual food is spoken of as Bread, and physical Bread is treated as the means of spiritual health; that water is treated as the instrument of regeneration, and spiritual teaching is called living water; that sometimes the physical touch is regarded as healing the spirit, and sometimes the spiritual touch as healing the body; in short, that Christ discerned a most intimate alliance between physical and spiritual agencies, in virtue of which the physical were often spiritual and the spiritual often physical; that he claimed the power to make the most ordinary constituents of the human body channels of spiritual life; and the most marvellous spiritual teachings equivalents for ordinary rest and nutrition. He recognized not only the working of the spirit on the flesh, but of the flesh on the spirit, and promised not only spiritual aid to overcome physical passions, but physical aid to overcome unspiritual passions. And in so doing, Christ did but follow the track of the natural life of man. What is more common than to find pure air restoring health to the spirit as well as pure social influences restoring health to the body? Does not the beauty of mountain scenery give a new zest to the very food we eat, and make it go further in nourishing the bodily tissues? Does not pure food give a new activity to the mind, and make it keener even in the life of prayer and of duty?

"But most men will admit at once that the reciprocal action of the spiritual on the material and of the material on the spiritual is the most certain and, perhaps some will say, the least mysterious of human phenomena, since if Mind creates matter, all material forces are but mental energies in disguise; and if Matter constitutes mind, mental energies are but material forces in disguise. In such apparently reciprocal influences of material and spiritual agencies, then, it will be said, there is not the vestige of the alleged Sacramental principle, which is not supposed to consist in the natural influence of the material on the spiritual, but in the supernatural transformation of material agencies which, while leaving them to act in their old material way, yet infuses them with a new life that not only affects the mind directly, but affects it also by purifying or refining the bodily organs. What rationalists deny is not the effect of material agencies in stimulating the spirit,—which they would of course steadily assert,—nor the effect of spiritual agencies in exciting the spirit,—but the possibility that by any spiritual process whatever a material agency could have its material effects so modified as to make the body a more pure and perfect organ of the spirit, in other words, to make it respond more easily to the government of the higher Christian impulses. They would admit that the habit of self-control would make the body a more manageable organ for the spirit; and again, that healthy physical habits would make it a more efficient instrument of every kind; but they would deny that the particles of food could be made to have any different effect, as particles of food, through any conceivable religious rite which might be performed, though they might concede that any high excitement of the nerves would probably disturb the bodily functions, and make their action *different*,—probably not healthier,—than it otherwise would be.

But is not that mere attempt to state the case accurately, **as** it is conceived by the rationalists, full of evidence that it **is** exceedingly difficult so to state it as to exclude all room for the proper Sacramental principle? They have to admit frankly that the same material substances act in most different fashions under different spiritual conditions;—only they would maintain that the changed spiritual conditions act through the nervous system of the recipient, and not through any transformation of the elements which pass into the body. Admitted, but is not this in its turn a distinction as refined and intangible as almost any theological distinction? Could any physiologist distinguish between an effect produced on the assimilation of food by the higher tension of the nerves **due** to spiritual feeling, and an effect produced by the modification of the substance received? An element once in the body, the discrimination between what is due to its action on the bodily organs and what is due to the action of the bodily organs on it, is surely almost inapprehensible, and quite evanescent? Supposing the body be really made a finer organ for the spirit by any internal change, suppose the inflammability of evil passions were diminished, and the impressibility to spiritual impulses were increased, is it not almost as childish and as unverifiable a refinement as any of which theologians have ever been guilty, to maintain that you can distinguish between what is due to the physical action of the food on the body, and what is due to the nervous action of the spirit or spirits on the food? No doubt it may be very fairly said that if anything of the Sacramental influence supposed to be exerted were really due to the bread and wine received, it would be only reasonable to assume that that influence would depend, as it does in the case of the air breathed in beautiful scenery for example (which doubtless has a more salutary effect on the body than equally good air breathed in uninteresting scenery), in great measure on the physical *amount* so received, whereas, as everybody knows, most of the believers in the Sacramental principle regard the minutest portions of the sacred elements as amply adequate to convey the new stream of spiritual life, and hold, therefore, that even though no material substance were taken at all, if the recipient *believed* that he had received the symbols of Divine life, the rite would have precisely the same physical and spiritual effect upon him as if he had really received them. Nor can we, of course, doubt that this is true. But the question which suggests itself is this,—whether, supposing it **to be true, as of** course it is, that it is not the elements received **which** effect anything, but only the divine influence of which **they** are such vivid symbolic channels, it may not **yet** be quite as much a physical as a spiritual change through which that divine influence operates. If beauty both of sight and sound acts, as it does, on the body by modulating the organs of sense, why may not the highest divine life mould the body directly, as well as through the slow influence of the mind upon **it? The** real essence of the Sacramental principle is, we imagine, contained in the assumption that **the divine life enters us** by physical as well as by spiritual channels; **and** for this purpose, of course, it matters **not at** all whether the Sacred Elements be but living symbols to our minds of that belief, **or** the actual channels of it. There seems **to us, at** all events, no sort of superstition in holding that,—independently of course of all sacredotal conditions,*— the rite which treats Christ's Body as the bread of life, does exert a very strange and spiritually-renovating influence on the human *body*,—does make the body, that is, a more perfect **and** delicate instrument of the human spirit. It is quite certain, at all events, that no Church, in which the Sacramental principle,—the principle that the spirit is spiritualized through the divine influence acting on the body as well as on the spirit,—has been deficient, has ever avoided at once the dangers of too exciting and fanatical a doctrine, of conscious " conversion," and also the danger of too cold a re-

---

* I cannot see the force of this reservation.

liance on " good works." The Sacramental principle and it alone has brought home to religious people the many different avenues, involuntary and unconscious as well as voluntary and conscious, physical as well as spiritual, by which the Spirit of God must enter man, if the character is to be really pervaded with divine influence. That principle alone guards adequately against morbid Calvinist broodings over the evidence of special grace, and cold Pelagian reliance on moral goodness. That exaltation of the common things of nature, which results from the teaching that divine life enters through the daily bread into the very tissues of the body, no less than through the Spirit of God into the conscience, prevents the relative overrating of the spiritual life as such, besides exerting a unique influence on the affections by the strictly personal relation to Christ into which it brings us."—(See 'Spectator,' June 15, 1872.)

Note D (p. 209).

The following eloquent passage is valuable, coming as it does, from an independent thinker like Mr. Goldwin Smith:—

"There are many peculiarities arising out of personal and historical circumstances, which are incident to the best human characters, and which would prevent any one of them from being universal or final as a type. But the Type set up in the Gospels as the Christian Type seems to have escaped all these peculiarities, and to stand out in unapproached purity as well as in unapproached perfection of moral excellence.

"The good moral characters which we see among men fall, speaking broadly, into two general classes; those which excite our reverence and those which excite our love. These two classes are essentially identical, since the object of our **reverence is** that elevation above selfish objects, that dignity, majesty, nobleness, appearance of moral strength which is produced by a disregard of selfish objects in comparison of those which are of a less selfish and therefore of a grander kind. But though essentially identical, they form, as it were, two hemispheres in the actual world of moral excellence; the noble and the amiable, or, in the language of moral taste, the grand and the beautiful. Being, however, essentially identical, they constantly tend to fusion in the human characters which are nearest to perfection, though, no human character being perfect, they are never actually fused. Now, if the type proposed in the Gospels for our imitation were characteristically noble or characteristically amiable, characteristically grand or characteristically beautiful, it might have great moral attractions, but it would not be universal or final. It would belong to one peculiar hemisphere of character, and even though man might not yet actually have transcended it, the ideal would lie beyond it; it would not remain for ever the mark and goal of our moral progress. But the fact is, it is neither characteristically noble and grand, nor characteristically amiable and beautiful; but both in an equal degree, perfectly and indistinguishably, the fusion of the two classes of qualities being complete, so that the mental eye, though it be strained to aching, cannot discern whether that on which it gazes be more the object of reverence or of love.

"There are differences again between the male and female character, under which, nevertheless, we divine that there lies a real identity, and a consequent tendency to fusion in the ultimate ideal. Had the Gospel type of character been stamped with the peculiar marks of either sex, we should have felt that there was an ideal free from those peculiarities beyond it. But this is not the case. It exhibits, indeed, the peculiarly male virtue of courage in the highest degree,

Q

and in the form in which it is most clear of mere animal impetuosity and most evidently a virtue; but this form is the one common to both sexes, as the annals of martyrdom prove. The Roman Catholics have attempted to consecrate a female type, that of the Virgin, by the side of that which they take to be characteristically male. But the result obviously is a mutilation of the original type, which really contained **all that** the other is supposed to supply; and the creation of a second type which has nothing distinctive, but is in its attributes, as well as in its history, merely **a** pale and partial reflection of the first.

"There is an equally notable absence of any of the peculiarities which attend particular callings and modes of life, and which, though so inevitable under the circumstances of human society that we have learnt to think them beauties, would disqualify a Character for being universal and the ideal. The Life depicted in the Gospel is one of pure beneficence, disengaged from all peculiar social circumstances, yet adapted to **all.** In vain would the Roman Catholic priest point to it as an example of a state like his own; the circumstances of Christ's life and mission repel any inferences of the kind.

"The Christian Type of Character, **if it** was constructed **by human** intellect, was constructed at the confluence of three races, the Jewish, the Greek, and **the** Roman, each of which had strong national peculiarities of its own. A single touch, a single taint of any one of those peculiarities, and the character would have been national, not universal; transient, not eternal; it might have been the highest character in history, but it would have been disqualified for being the ideal. Supposing it to have been human, whether it were the effort of a real man to attain moral excellence, or a moral imagina**tion of** the writers of the Gospels, the chances, surely, were infinite against its escaping any tincture of the fanaticism, formalism, and exclusiveness of the Jew, of the political pride of the Roman, of the intellectual pride of the Greek. Yet it has entirely escaped them all.

"Historical circumstances affect character sometimes directly, sometimes by way of reaction. The formalism of the Pharisees might have been expected to drive any character with which it was brought into collision into the opposite extreme of laxity; yet no such effect can be discerned. Antinomianism is clearly a deflection from the Christian pattern, and the offspring of a subsequent age.

"The political circumstances of Judea, as a country suffering from the oppression of foreign conquerors, were calculated to produce in the oppressed Jews either insurrectionary violence (which was constantly breaking out) or the dull apathy of Oriental submission. But the Life which is the example of Christians escaped both these natural impressions. It was an active and decisive attack on the evils of the age; but the attack was directed not against political tyranny or its agents, but against the moral corruption which was its source.

"There are certain qualities which are not virtues in themselves, but are made virtues by time and circumstance, and with their times and circumstances pass away; yet, while they last, are often naturally and almost necessarily esteemed above those virtues which are most real and universal. These factitious virtues are the offspring for the most part of early states of society, and the attendant narrowness of moral vision. Such was headlong valour among the Northmen. Such was, and is, punctilious hospitality among the tribes of the Desert. Such was the fanatical patriotism of the ancients, which remained a virtue, while the nation remained the largest sphere of moral sympathy known to man,—his vision not having yet embraced his kind. The taint of one of these factitious and temporary virtues would, in the eye of historical philosophy, have been as fatal to the perfection and universality of a type of character as the taint of a positive vice. Not only the fellow-countrymen, but the companions and Apostles of Christ were, by the account of the Gospels, imbued with that Jewish patriotism, the fanatical intensity of which disgusted even the ancient world. They desired to convert their Master into a patriot chief and to turn His universal mission into one for the peculiar benefit of His own race. Had they succeeded in doing so, even in the slightest degree,—or to take a different hypothesis, had those who constructed the mythical character of Christ admitted into it the slightest tinge of a **quality** which they could hardly, without a miracle, distinguish from a real virtue,—the time would have arrived when, the vision of man being enlarged, and his affection for his country becoming subordinate to his affection for his kind, the Christian Type would have grown antiquated, and would have been left behind in the progress of history towards a higher and ampler ideal. But such is not the case. A just affection for country may indeed find its prototype in Him who wept over the impending destruction of Jerusalem, and who offered the Gospel first to the Jew: but His character stands clear of the narrow partiality which it is the tendency of advancing civilization to discard. From exaggerated patriotism and from exaggerated cosmopolitanism the Christian Example is equally free.

"Asceticism, again, if it has never been a virtue, even under exceptional circumstances, is very easily mistaken for one, and has been almost universally mistaken for one in the, East. There are certain states of society,—such, for example as that which the Western monks were called upon to evangelize and civilize by their exertions,—in which **it is difficult to deny the usefulness and merit of an ascetic life. But** had the type of character set before us in the Gospel been ascetic, our social experience must have discarded it in the long run; as our moral experience would have discarded **it** in the long run had it been connected with those formal observances into the consecration of which asceticism almost inevitably falls. But the type of character set before us in the Gospels is not ascetic, though it is the highest exhibition **of** self-denial. Nor is it connected with formal observances, though, for reasons which are of universal and permanent validity, it provisionally condescends to the **observances** established in the Jewish Church. The character of the Essenes, as painted by Josephus, which seems to outvie the Christian character in purity and self-denial, is tainted both with asceticism and formalism, and though a lofty and pure conception, could not have been accepted by man as permanent and universal.

"Cast your eyes over the human characters of history, and observe to how great an extent the most soaring and eccentric of them are the creatures of their country and their **age.** Examine the most poetic of human visions, and mark how closely they are connected, either by way of direct emanation or of reaction, with the political **and** social circumstances amidst which they were conceived; how manifestly the Utopia of Plato is an emanation from the Spartan commonwealth, how manifestly the Utopia of Rousseau is **a re**action against the artificial society of Paris. What likelihood, then, was there that the imagination of a peasant **of** Galilee would spring at a bound beyond place and time, **and** create a type of character perfectly distinct in its personality, yet entirely free from all that entered into the special personalities of the age; a type which satisfies us as entirely as it satisfied him, and which, as far as we can see or imagine, will satisfy all men to the end of time.

"The character of Mahomet, and the character which is represented by the name of Buddha, were no doubt great improvements in their day on anything which had preceded them among the races out of which they arose. But the character of Mahomet was deeply tainted with fierce Arab enterprise, that of Buddha with languid Eastern resignation: and all progress among the nations by which these types were consecrated has long since come to an end.

"M. Comte has constructed for his sect a whimsical Calendar of historic characters, in imitation of the Roman Catholic Calendar of Saints. Each month and each day is given to the historic representative of some great achievement of Humanity. Theocracy is there, represented by Moses, ancient poetry by Homer, ancient philosophy by Aristotle, Roman Civilization by Cæsar, Feudal Civilization by Charlemagne, and so forth; the ancient Saints having their modern counterparts, and each having a crowd of minor Saints belonging to the same department of historical progress in his train. Catholicism is there, represented somewhat strangely by St. Paul instead of St. Peter. Christianity is not there: neither is Christ. It cannot be asserted that a person circumstantially mentioned by Tacitus is less historical than Prometheus, Orpheus, and Numa, who all appear in this Calendar; and the allegation that there is no Christianity but Catholicism, and that St. Paul, not Christ, was its real founder, is too plainly opposed to facts to need discussion. The real reason, I apprehend, is that Christianity and its Author, though unquestionably historical, have no peculiar historical characteristics, and no limited place in history. And are we to believe that men whose culture was so small, and whose range of vision was necessarily so limited as those of the first Christians, produced a character which a French atheist philosopher of the nineteenth century finds himself unable to treat as human, and place, in its historical relations, among the human benefactors of the race? Do you imagine that it is from respect for the feelings of Christian society that M. Comte hesitates to put this name into his Calendar, beside the names of Cæsar and Frederic the Great? The treatise in which the Calendar is given opens with an announcement that M. Comte, by a decisive proclamation, made at what he is pleased to style the memorable conclusion of his course of lectures, has inaugurated the reign of Humanity and put an end to the reign of God.

"The essence of man's moral nature, clothed with a personality so vivid and intense as to excite through all ages the most intense affection, yet divested of all those peculiar characteristics, the accidents of place and time, by which human personalities are marked, what other notion than this can philosophy form of Divinity manifest on earth?"—('Lectures on Modern History,' Lect. pp. 15–22.)

www.ingramcontent.com/pod-product-compliance
Lightning Source LLC
Chambersburg PA
CBHW021814230426
43669CB00008B/746